M000106755

The purpose of this study guide is to provide supplemental educational material. It is not intended as a substitute or replacement of PIECING ME TOGETHER.

Published by SuperSummary, www.supersummary.com

ISBN – 9781702429764

For more information or to learn about our complete library of study guides, please visit http://www.supersummary.com

Please submit any comments, corrections, or questions to:
http://www.supersummary.com/support/

TABLE OF CONTENTS

Piecing Me Together by Renée Watson is a young adult novel published in 2017. In 2018, it won the Coretta Scott King Award from the American Library Award Association and was named a Newbery Honor Book by the Association for Library Service to Children. The novel comprises 76 chapters, each of which is given a bilingual title in English and Spanish. For example, Chapter 1 is titled "*español* - Spanish language," and Chapter 2 is titled "*tener éxito* - to succeed." Throughout the book, certain chapters are highly stylized, one-page fragments that fall outside the general trajectory of the narrative—these chapters mirror protagonist Jade Butler's preferred medium of self-expression: collaging.

Piecing Me Together explores themes of intersectionality, self- and community-based advocacy, and the unique experience of coming of age as a black girl. It also celebrates the black experience and self-expression through art. The book exposes how certain well-intentioned programs like Woman to Woman, meant to empower the disadvantaged, actually disempower and demean them; as Woman to Woman undergoes a transformation over the course of the book, *Piecing Me Together* offers a vision of what a true, authentic mentorship organization might look like.

Plot Summary

Set in modern-day Oregon, *Piecing Me Together* tells the story of Jade Butler, an African American high school student growing up in North Portland, an impoverished area of the city of Portland. Jade is a scholarship student at the elite private high school St. Francis, where the well-meaning school administrators—including her guidance counselor, Mrs. Parker—give her many opportunities. Jade is studying Spanish, and she dreams of one day traveling the world. St. Francis has a study abroad program, and Jade hopes to be nominated for the program so that she can travel to Costa Rica. Jade expresses herself through art and her preferred medium is collaging. As a collage artist, she takes everyday objects—pamphlets, photos, newspaper clippings—and transforms them into things of beauty.

During Jade's junior year at St. Francis, Mrs. Parker encourages her to join a mentorship program for African American girls called Woman to Woman, which pairs each student with a St. Francis alumna. Jade's mentor is Maxine, a black woman from an upper-middle-class background. Jade and Maxine form an uneasy relationship, but Jade is critical of some of Maxine's behaviors: Maxine is distracted by her relationship with a deadbeat ex-boyfriend; she was late to their first-ever Woman to Woman meeting; but most of all, she treats Jade as an object of pity who will help give meaning to her life.

Meanwhile, Jade forms a friendship with Sam, a white girl who rides the same bus to school. Sam is from Northeast Portland, a poor, primarily white section of the city. While Jade and Sam share an understanding based on socioeconomic class and their relationship to money, there is a huge divide in their understanding of race. Jade's life is peppered with all sorts of racist incidents: She is seen as "unruly" by a school lunch lady; she is ejected from a store in the mall for just browsing; she is looked over by her Spanish professor for St. Francis's study abroad program.

The turning point in the novel comes when Jade begins voicing her needs: She lets Maxine know that she feels ignored; she tells the founder of Woman to Woman that the program would be more effective if it gave the mentees more practical advice and stopped treating them as objects of charity; and she tells Sam it is hurtful that Sam does not believe Jade faces racism on a daily basis.

The novel concludes with Jade taking control of her own future. With the support of Maxine and the newly-transformed Woman to Woman, Jade combines her passion for collaging with her desire for social justice. Shaken by the recent violence against a young black student named Natasha Ramsey, Jade and her best friend, Lee Lee, raise awareness (and money to pay for hospital bills) for Natasha by putting on a community art show. Maxine offers to hold the event at her sister's art gallery, and the event is a fantastic success. By the end of the novel, Woman to Woman has transformed at its core: The organization no longer treats its mentees as problems needing to be "fixed," but listens to them and approaches their needs with respect.

Chapters 1-20

Chapter 1 Summary: *"español* - Spanish language"

The novel opens with a fragmented, first-person statement from an unknown narrator: "I am learning to speak. To give myself a way out. A way in" (1). The reader knows nothing about the speaker or the context—it is a disembodied declaration having to do with speech and escape.

Chapter 2 Summary: *"tener éxito* - to succeed"

The reader is introduced to Jade Butler, the first-person speaker and narrator of the novel. Jade is just beginning her junior year at St. Francis High, a private school in Portland, Oregon. One of the first facts the reader learns about Jade is that she is studying the Spanish language: "When I learned the Spanish word for *succeed,* I thought it was kind of ironic that the word *exit* is embedded in it" (2). St. Francis is one of the best private schools in Portland, and Jade is only able to attend with the support of a full scholarship. St. Francis is located in a different part of Portland from where Jade lives, and she must take a long bus ride to school.

Unlike her classmates at St. Francis—who, for the most part, are wealthy and white—Jade is African American and her mother struggles to provide for her and her family on a meager salary. Jade's mother is a home health aide for an elderly white woman by the name of Ms. Louise, having been fired from her previous job for stealing: "Mom used to work as a housekeeper at Emanuel Hospital, but she got fired because she was caught stealing supplies. She sometimes brought home blankets and the small lotions that are given to patients" (3).

It is the evening, and Jade is in her room trying to choose an outfit to wear for school the next day: "So here I am, trying to pick out something to wear that doesn't look like I'm trying too hard to impress or that I don't care about how I look" (3). Jade's mother enters the room and tells her that the following morning she will not be there to see Jade off to school. Jade's mother then launches into what Jade refers to as "the Talk": "Every year since I started at St. Francis, Mom comes to my room the night before school starts to give me the Talk" (4). "The Talk" is a plea for Jade to make friends at St. Francis, since Jade's mom feels that Jade has been isolating herself. Jade's mother worries because Jade acts as if she "can't survive" if she is not "joined together at the hip" (5) with Lee Lee, her best friend from the neighborhood. Lee Lee goes to the local high school, called Northside, which is where Jade would have gone had she not been accepted to St. Francis. Jade's mother also reminds her that the next day she has a meeting with Mrs. Parker, her guidance counselor at school. Jade is excited for the meeting: "This is the year that teachers selected students to volunteer in a foreign country and do service learning projects. [...] She [Mrs. Parker] knew from my application essay that I wanted to take Spanish and that I wanted to travel" (6). Mrs. Parker always has some opportunity—a scholarship, a program, a class—at the ready for Jade, and Jade wishes she were in a position to turn them down: "But girls like me, with coal skin and hula-hoop hips, whose mommas barely make enough money to keep food in the house, have to take opportunities every chance we get" (7).

As Jade's mother leaves Jade's bedroom, she asks if Jade needs anything from the grocery store. Jade says she wrote an item on the list tacked to the fridge, and Jade's mother laughs and says she thought it was E.J. who wrote "mint chocolate chip ice cream." E.J., the reader learns, is Jade's mother's younger brother, who lives with them. E.J. dropped out of college and now is a local deejay with no real plans to return to school. Jade's mother promises that, if she has enough money left over, she will get the ice cream. Jade is not optimistic that she will come through with her promise: "I finish getting ready for school, thinking to myself that I know all about Mom's promises. She does her best to make them, but they are fragile and break easily" (8).

Chapter 3 Summary: *"dejar - to leave"*

Jade leaves for school early the following day. She takes the 35 bus, which winds through a "maze of houses that all look like one another, like sisters who are not twins but everyone thinks they are" (9). Jade lives in an area of North Portland referred to as "The New Columbia," which has a reputation for being a dangerous, impoverished area—it is located far from Jade's wealthy high school. On the ride, Jade reflects on various parts of her life: how she's able to find beauty even in the ugliest of things, how her mother stayed in Portland only because she gave birth to Jade, how her father re-married a white woman after he and Jade's mother divorced.

In Northeast Portland, a girl about Jade's age gets on the bus and begins reading a book: "A white girl gets on and goes to sit in the first empty seat she sees. She has dark brown hair pulled back and twisted into a mess of a ponytail" (11). Jade wonders if this girl goes to St. Francis, and when she exits at the same stop as Jade, it is clear that she does. The girl walks quickly into the crowd of students at the school before Jade has a chance to ask her if she is a new student. Jade looks out at the student body and notices "a few sections of color" among them, naming the few other African American students who attend St. Francis:

"There's Rose, one of the other black girls here, who I thought I'd become friends with […] Then there's Josiah—the tech nerd who somehow in a place like this is one of the coolest, most popular guys in the school" (12).

Inside, Josiah sees Jade and stops her in the hallway. He invites her to lunch, but Jade says she cannot make it; secretly, it is because she is can't afford to eat out for lunch. Both Rose and Josiah come from rich families, and Jade reflects on the differences in their upbringings, despite all being from African American families. Jade eats her lunch in the cafeteria, thinking about her upcoming meeting with Mrs. Parker, who will give Jade more information about St. Francis's foreign service learning program: "[N]othing would make me miss this meeting with Mrs. Parker. I can't wait to find out what country we're going to, what the service learning project will be" (13). Jade is ⊂HR eager to travel and therefore is excited to learn about the program.

Chapter 4 Summary: *"querer - to want"*

Later that day, Jade spots the girl again: "I am sitting in Mr. Flores's Spanish class, and I see that the girl from the bus is here too" (14). For a group project, Jade is partnered with Kennedy, who is "one of the few black girls" in her grade. Jade secretly refers to Kennedy as "Glamour Girl" because Kennedy is always "applying lip gloss or fixing her hair" (14). They are not friends.

When the lunch bell rings, Jade makes her way to Mrs. Parker's office: "Like most of the adults in this school, Mrs. Parker is white. I imagine her to be a fun grandmother to the three boys in the pictures that decorate her office" (15). Jade anticipates that Mrs. Parker will tell Jade that she has been nominated for St. Francis's study abroad program.

CH12

Jade desperately wants to travel the world; she longs to go to Costa Rica or somewhere in Latin America where she can practice her Spanish language skills. Instead, Mrs. Parker slides a brochure to Jade across her desk for an organization called Woman to Woman, a mentorship program for African American girls. Mrs. Parker informs Jade that 12 girls from high schools throughout Portland have been chosen to join Woman to Woman, and that Jade is one of them. Each girl will be paired with a mentor for the two-year program, at the end of which, so long as the student's GPA is a 3.5 or above, each girl will receive a scholarship to any Oregon college.

[handwritten left margin: EQ *]*
[handwritten left margin: white woman (PARKER) hands a brochure for "help" to the presumed poor and possibly struggling black student — Instead of giving her the TRAVEL INFORMATION/ PROGRAM! *]*

Though Jade is disappointed that she has no news from Mrs. Parker on the study abroad program, she reluctantly agrees to participate in Woman to Woman. Jade completes a brief questionnaire for the program with her full name ("Jade Butler"), favorite color ("yellow"), and hobbies ("collaging"), but when asked what she expects to get out of the program, she doesn't answer: "I leave that one blank" (20).

Chapter 5 Summary: *"promesa* - promise"

When Jade arrives home from school, she senses her mother's presence in the house immediately: "Mom's scent hugs me as soon as I get in the door" (21). Jade's mother is resting on her twin bed; Jade observes that she did not take off her work clothes before falling asleep in front of the TV.

[handwritten left margin: FIG *]*

Jade goes into the kitchen and sees empty brown paper bags strewn all over the countertop—she knows that her mother went to the grocery store. Jade checks to see if her mother kept her promise to get the ice cream Jade requested: "And in the freezer: family value-size ground

9

beef, frozen pizzas. And in the way, way back—ice cream. Mint chocolate chip" (21).

Chapter 6 Summary: *"historia* - history"

Lee Lee and Jade compare their first days back at school: "Lee Lee comes over after school, and over bowls of mint chocolate chip ice cream, we swap stories about our first day" (22). Lee Lee tells Jade how much she likes her new history teacher, Mrs. Phillips, particularly because she offers a new take on American history. Lee Lee says that "she's all about teaching stuff we don't necessarily learn in our textbooks" (23) and that the class is now learning about York, the black slave who accompanied Lewis and Clark on their famous journey. York was a good hunter and helped navigate the crew, along with Native American Sacagawea, safely to Oregon. Rarely discussed in conventional American history, York was "just as important" (23) to the expedition as Lewis and Clark but does not get credit for being such a vital member of the expedition, claims Lee Lee's teacher.

Lee Lee starts discussing high school gossip—"who's broken up, who's gotten back together"—but Jade is still thinking about what Lee Lee is learning in Mrs. Phillips's history class: "The whole time Lee Lee is talking, I am thinking about York and Sacagawea, wondering how they must have felt having a form of freedom but no real power" (24).

Chapter 7 Summary: *"arte* - art"

After Lee Lee leaves, Jade works on an art project. Collaging is Jade's preferred medium. The materials she uses in this instance are a copy of the 35 bus schedule and an old issue of *St. John's Review*, her community newsletter. She cuts them into bits, transforming them: "I am ripping and cutting. Gluing and pasting. Rearranging reality, redefining, covering, disguising" (25). As she works, Jade thinks back on her conversation with Lee Lee about York; she also thinks about the parallels between Mrs. Parker and the British colonists who pillaged the Native Americans in the era of Lewis and Clark.

EQ

Chapter 8 Summary: "*algo en común* - something in common"

Jade is on the bus to school, observing the girl from the day before: "The Book Girl gets on the bus again" (27). When a rowdy passenger boards the bus, playing his music loudly, Jade and Book Girl lock eyes in a shared look of irritation and understanding. Jade motions for Book Girl to come sit by her. Book Girl takes the seat next to Jade; she introduces herself as Sam. Jade tells Sam that she lives in North Portland. Sam lives near Peninsula Park, which is slightly closer than North Portland, but still very far from St. Francis.

Since Sam is new at the school, Jade gives Sam advice on how to navigate St. Francis: "As we ride to school together, I make sure to tell her the shortcuts to get around the crowded hallways. I let her know which teachers she should stay away from at all costs and which ones to get to know even if she doesn't have their classes" (28). Before getting off the bus, Sam suggests that she and Jade eat lunch together.

Chapter 9 Summary: "*esperar* - to wait"

Jade and Sam become fast friends: "September has come and gone. My daily routine is riding the bus in the morning and eating lunch with Sam" (30). One evening after school,

Jade attends her first Woman to Woman meeting at a library in Northeast Portland.

After school Jade heads to the library, where people are starting to gather for the Woman to Woman meeting: "When I get to the library, groups of women are huddled in circles making small talk" (31). Jade is greeted by an organizer and given a nametag; she is also told that her mentor, named Maxine, has not arrived yet.

Maxine still has not arrived when Sabrina, the founder of Woman to Woman, stands at the front of the stage to make her welcoming remarks. Sabrina discusses the reasons why she started the program: "I started this program because I believe in the power of sisterhood. We girls are often overlooked as if our needs are not important. And, well, I got tired of complaining, and wanted to do something about it" (32). Sabrina says that they will have fun, but they will also learn strategies for success and overcoming challenges. Next, Sabrina leads the group in an icebreaker exercise: Each mentor and mentee stand together and, one by one, they all go around the room and give their names. Each person must give an adjective that describes her and that also begins with the same letter as her first name—for example, a woman in the group calls herself "Hilarious Hillary" (34). Jade's mentor, Maxine, still has not arrived when the game begins, and Jade is upset by her absence: "I think of names for my mentor: Missing Maxine, Mediocre Maxine, Mean Maxine" (34). Irritated with Maxine and the "stupid" getting-to-know-you game, Jade slips out the back of the library and takes the bus home. When Jade enters her house, her mother can tell that something is upsetting Jade: "She [Jade's mom] is good at reading minds, reading the room, at having a feeling that won't go away" (35). Jade tells her mother that her mentor never showed up to the meeting and so she left. Jade's mother asks why Jade did not speak up for herself by saying something to the organizers.

Jade also reveals in this chapter why her uncle E.J. is living with her and her mother: He dropped out of college a year earlier after one of his best friends fell victim to gun violence. Jade notes: "Nothing's been the same since then. I think Mom only hears what she wants to hear, sees what she wants to see when it comes to her baby brother. Mom knows E.J. is not fine" (35).

Chapter 10 Summary: *"presenter* - to introduce"

Jade calls Lee Lee when she arrives home after Woman to Woman: "I am on the phone, talking to Lee Lee, telling her everything that did and didn't happen at the Woman to Woman welcome meeting" (38). When Lee Lee and Jade hang up the phone, there is knock at the door and Jade peers out the window to see a woman standing there:

> [O]n a second look, I think maybe she's lost and needs directions. She's way too pretty to be here for E.J. Her hair is crinkled and wild, all over the place—but on purpose. She's somewhere in the middle of thick and big-boned. I want to look like that. Instead I'm just plump. I open the door (39).

The woman introduces herself as Maxine. She apologizes for not showing up to the meeting but explains that "[a] ton of stuff happened" (39) that prevented her from attending. Jade reluctantly accepts the explanation. Maxine gives Jade a gift bag, and Jade wonders if Maxine is trying to "buy [her] forgiveness" (40). Inside are art supplies: colored paper, oil pastels, a sketchbook.

Maxine asks to know more about Jade's art. Jade explains, "Well, I like to take things that people don't usually find beautiful and make them beautiful. Like, blocks here in the Villa, or sometimes people in my neighborhood. I don't know. I get ideas from everywhere" (41). Jade shows Maxine a collection of her collages, including one she made to commemorate the death of Lee Lee's grandmother. The collage is made from bits of fabric from Lee Lee's grandmother's handkerchiefs and clippings from the funeral program. Maxine compliments Jade's work and tells her that she is going to tell her sister, Mia, who owns an art gallery, about Jade's collages.

Maxine's phone rings and she excuses herself to take the call. When Maxine returns her attention to Jade, they discuss St. Francis and continue to get to know one another through small talk. Jade asks Maxine if she was in the Woman to Woman program, and Maxine says no, though when Mrs. Parker approached her about the program Maxine was interested as a way of "giving back" (44). Maxine pulls her phone from her pocket, checking her text messages. E.J. enters the living room and, to Jade's surprise, he recognizes Maxine: "My mentor knows my uncle? I'm not sure how to feel about this" (45). It turns out that E.J. is friends with Jon, Maxine's ex-boyfriend; E.J. says that Jon told him about his and Maxine's fight earlier today, but E.J. is confident that they will get back together. Maxine says that this break-up is final, alluding to a pattern of multiple break-ups with Jon. Meanwhile, Jade wonders if this "drama" with her ex-boyfriend is what prevented Maxine from attending Woman to Woman that evening. After Maxine leaves, Jade questions whether joining Woman to Woman was a good idea, given Maxine's questionable behavior with her ex-boyfriend: "All of this has me wondering, what have I gotten myself into? Has me wondering, what is this woman really going to teach me?" (46).

Chapter 11 Summary: *"buenos días* - good morning"

The next day before school, Jade shows her mother the expensive art supplies that Maxine gave. Jade's mother looks at the shared dry erase board calendar in their kitchen, which they use to keep track of the family schedule. She notes that Jade has a busy week: "On Monday I'm staying after school for a National Honor Society meeting. Wednesday and Thursday I tutor Josiah, and Friday night there's a one-on-one mentoring outing with Maxine" (47). Jade's mother tells her that "[i]t'll be worth it" (47), referring to Jade's rigorous weekly schedule. Jade's mother says that she wants to meet Maxine before their one-on-one outing; she does not like the idea of her daughter going out with a stranger, even if she is a mentor with Woman to Woman. Jade leaves for school.

CHR
Mother
is
Protective
and
cautious

Chapter 12 Summary: *"amiga* - female friend"

After school, Jade goes to Sam's house. Sam lives with her grandparents and, before arriving, she gives Jade "disclaimers and warnings" about what Jade will encounter at her house: "Okay, so my house is small and kind of cluttered because my grandparents refuse to throw anything away" (50). Sam also tells Jade about her grandparents' health problems, particularly her grandmother's Alzheimer's, which makes her "moody" and "forgetful" (51).

When they arrive at the house, Sam shouts inside to announce their arrival: "Grandma, it's me, Sam. I'm home. I have a friend with me" (51). Sam's grandmother is watching the news on the TV and does not acknowledge

Sam and Jade when they enter the room. Sam's grandfather calls the girls into the kitchen. He greets Jade and asks her where she lives, and when she replies North Portland, Sam's grandmother shouts from the other room: "Nothing but hillbillies, blacks, and Mexicans over there!" (52). Sam mouths "I'm so sorry" to Jade as her grandmother continues her tirade about the neighborhood. Sam's grandfather explains that the Franklin family has lived in Northeast Portland for many years and seen the neighborhood dramatically change over the last decade. He alludes to the fact that the neighborhood demographics are changing—namely, with more black families moving there—and that the rest of the neighborhood (presumably, white people) is not adjusting easily.

Jade and Sam head to Sam's room to practice their Spanish. Midway through their studying, Sam's grandfather enters the room to say that Sam's mother is on the phone and wants to speak with her. Sam quickly takes the call, saying that she is fine and needs to get back to studying. Jade is surprised at Sam's distant relationship with her mother, whom she only sees once a month. Instead of continuing their studying, they talk about their families, their experiences as poor kids at St. Francis, and how privileged they are compared to their peers from their neighborhoods. Above all, they share the feeling of being "stuck in the middle" (58), in Sam's words. Jade says how happy she is to have Sam as a friend now.

Chapter 13 Summary: "*hija* - daughter"

It is early Sunday morning and Jade is waiting for Maxine to arrive at her mother's home so they can go out for brunch to celebrate Jade's upcoming birthday. Maxine was supposed to take Jade out for dinner last Friday, but she needed to cancel unexpectedly. Jade's mother asks why she is up so early. Jade explains that Maxine is coming by so that they can "do brunch" to celebrate her birthday, and Jade's mother scoffs, "*Do* brunch? You mean go to brunch? […] That woman has you talking like her already, huh?" (60). Jade's mother is angry that Jade did not tell her about this outing beforehand, in addition to being upset with Maxine for not getting her permission first. Jade's mother forbids her from going.

Doesn't Like Maxine

When Maxine rings the doorbell, Jade's mother opens the door and informs her that Jade cannot go to brunch with her. Furthermore, she tells Maxine that she must get her permission before making any more plans with Jade. Maxine apologizes, and Jade's mother invites her in for a brief visit with Jade.

Jade takes Maxine into her room and shows her the collage that she's been working on: It is about York, the slave who helped guide Lewis and Clark. Before Maxine leaves, she tells Jade's mother that she would like to take Jade to a bookstore downtown and purchase a few art books, remarking that Jade is very talented. Jade's mother says that Jade is allowed to go to the bookstore with Maxine the following weekend.

Chapter 14 Summary: "*feliz cumpleaños* - happy birthday"

SET

It is Jade's birthday and her mother is making Jade's favorite breakfast to celebrate: "I wake up to the smell of pancakes and bacon" (65). At the breakfast table, Jade tells her mother that she plans on spending the day with Lee Lee and Sam. She also mentions that her father is going to come by the house that night to drop off a gift.

Jade's mother goes to work, leaving Jade alone at home. As Jade gets dressed, Lee Lee calls to say that she got into an argument with her aunt, and so she is "on punishment" (67) and will not be able to see Jade for her birthday. Sam calls shortly after and says that she is sick and will not be able to join Jade either. Jade spends the rest of the afternoon watching TV, feeling sad that she must spend her birthday alone. Jade's dad does not come to drop off the gift, nor *CHR ?* does her call.

Jade is abandoned by her dad AND Society ?

Around eleven o'clock, Jade goes to her room and puts on her pajamas. She fights back tears as she lies on her bed listening to music. E.J. knocks on her door just as Jade is falling asleep and tells her to follow him into the kitchen. E.J. offers her a piece of cheesecake, saying that she "can't go to bed without some birthday dessert" (68).

Chapter 15 Summary: *"el pelo* - hair"

Chapter 15 is a brief, one-page vignette that portrays a small, quiet moment in Jade's life: It is a Sunday and Jade is at home relaxing. She has taken her braids out: "My black cotton hovers over me like a cloud. I'd never wear my hair like this to school, but today is Sunday and I'm home" (69). Jade's mother enters the house, takes off her shoes after a long day, and sighs.

FIG — Interesting way she chooses to describe her own hair

Chapter 16 Summary: *"regalo* - gift"

Jade's birthday weekend is over, and she makes her way to school on a windy, rainy morning. Sam is not on the bus that day, Jade notices.

Jade is greeted at school by Josiah, who wishes her a happy birthday. Jade is confused, as she does not know how her fellow students are aware that it was her birthday. When she rounds the hallway corner toward her locker, she sees Sam standing there: "She [Sam] is at my locker—only it doesn't look like my locker, because there are balloons and an oversized card taped on it. I walk faster, and when I get to her, she holds her arms out and hugs me" (71). Sam apologizes for missing Jade's birthday, but Jade has already forgiven her—she is delighted with Sam's surprise.

Chapter 17 Summary: *"mi padre* - my father"

That day after school, Jade goes to her father's home, where he greets her with a gift: "Dad goes into his bedroom and brings out two boxes. One has a digital camera in it, the other a mini photo printer" (72). Jade's father apologizes for missing her on her birthday—he offers the excuse that "[s]omething came up" (72), and Jade tells him he could have called. He claims that his cell phone died, and Jade makes a face that indicates her feeling that that is a subpar excuse. Finally, Jade's father relents and says that there is "no good reason" why he did not see her, and he apologizes again for hurting his "queen" (73).

Jade immediately starts taking photos with her new camera. She takes a couple of her father, and then they head to the kitchen to eat Chinese leftovers. Jade's father asks her how she is doing in school; she replies that she is studying Spanish and loves it, because she loves studying language. When he asks her why, she says it is because it makes her feel "powerful" (74). Jade reminds her father that he was the one to tell her how important it was for her to read, because it was once illegal for African Americans to learn how to read—she thinks that is a big reason why she feels that language is so powerful.

Chapter 18 Summary: *"fotografiar* - photograph"

Another one-page vignette details the various pictures that Jade takes with her new camera of the everyday life that surrounds her: "On the way home from Dad's I take as many photos as I can: Naked branches and tree trunks. Fallen leaves. A little girl falling asleep in her mother's arms on the bus" (75). The chapter closes with Jade turning the camera to face her, taking a self-portrait.

Chapter 19 Summary: *"libros* - books"

Maxine takes Jade to Powell's bookstore, and Jade is smitten despite having had reservations initially: "'This place feels magical,' I say to Maxine. When she first told me she was bringing me to a bookstore, I wasn't that excited to go" (76). Maxine informs a salesperson—who is a "short tan woman with a kinky Afro" (76)—that Jade is an artist, specifically a collagist, and that they are looking for books of inspiration from other black collagists. The salesperson suggests a book on the work of Romare Bearden and another on Mickalene Thomas. Jade is enthralled: "I am looking through the book, staring at these brown women and their faces that are pieced together with different shades of brown, different-size features, all mismatched yet perfectly puzzled together to make them whole beings" (77). Maxine pays for the books and says that Jade can thank her by using them as inspiration to make "great art" (78).

Chapter 20 Summary: *"doce* - twelve"

Chapter 20 is another one-page fragment, in stream-of-consciousness style, in which Jade ruminates on Woman to Woman and the number 12: "There are twelve girls who've been selected for the Woman to Woman mentorship program. Twelve seeds. Twelve prayers. Twelve daughters. Twelve roots" (79).

Chapters 1-20 Analysis

Piecing Me Together is written from the first-person perspective of Jade, the protagonist of the book. One of the core themes of *Piecing Me Together* is identity—specifically, stitching together and making sense of a fragmented, intersectional identity composed of many different parts—and the intimate, first-person perspective is crucial to the exploration of this theme.

"Intersectionality" is a sociological term that refers to the interconnected identity categories that make up an individual's identity. This term is often used to discuss and understand the ways in which different categories of identity—such as race or gender—are affected by systems of cultural oppression. African Americans are more likely to experience discrimination than white people in the United States, while women are more likely to experience gender discrimination than men. "Intersectionality" is a useful concept for unpacking the experiences of someone who faces multiple forms of cultural discrimination, such as a black woman. Being an African American is just one of several identifying features that inform Jade's overall experience at St. Francis and in the world at large. Jade's blackness, taken together with her class, gender, and size—her "hula-hoop hips" (7)—are all elements that shape and inform her identity, and *Piecing Me Together* examines the ways in which these parts of her identity come together to affect Jade's overall life experience.

Through the character of Jade, and how she interacts with those around her, Watson examines the numerous ways different kinds of identifying features intersect, shaping

Jade's perception of the world. For example, at St. Francis, Jade is one of the few black students within a mostly white, wealthy student body. Of the black students, many are from upper-middle-class families, and Jade knows that due to their class difference, they will have a fundamentally different view of the world. In Chapter 2, when a teacher asks whom society takes for granted and a student responds "her housekeeper," Jade explains: "I actually looked across the room at the only other black girl in the class, and she was raising her hand saying, 'She took my answer,' and so I knew we'd probably never make eye contact about anything" (5). In addition to race, a person's size might influence the way they carry themselves in the world. Jade is heavyset and that affects the way she behaves, based on how others perceive her. For example, in Chapter 4, Jade is embarrassed of her growling stomach: "I stare at the mints, and my stomach growls. Loud. I wish I could silence it. Big girls can't have growling stomachs" (15).

Socioeconomic status is another major component of Jade's identity, and the book explores how class influences a person's life experience. Jade's life is shaped by her family's lack of money and the burden that comes with financial insecurity. Even mundane experiences will be different compared to someone with wealth. When Jade's family dines out, they usually opt to eat at a buffet so they can secure extra food to take home for future meals: "This is something I learned from Mom. Whenever we go out to eat, we usually have dinner at an all-you-can-eat place, like Izzy's or Old Country Buffet" (32).

In these chapters, Watson introduces the reader to the book's primary characters: Jade; her mother; her uncle E.J.; her Women to Woman mentor, Maxine; and her new friend, Sam. Jade has felt very alone at St. Francis as one of the only African American students there on scholarship, and her friendship with Sam seems to offer Jade the promise of true companionship and an ally at St. Francis. Sam is white, but she has a similar socioeconomic background to Jade, and the girls share a tacit bond over a desire to escape their confining financial circumstances: "I am full of questions about her. I wonder what Sam is exiting from. She must be coming from something" (29).

Another parallel between Jade and Sam is a sense of embarrassment around their homes: Like Jade in Chapter 10 when Maxine comes to visit, Sam offers a number of warnings and disclaimers to Jade before they spend the afternoon at her grandparents' home in Chapter 12. Also like Jade, Sam does not feel that she is getting what she needs from the support services at St. Francis. Jade wants to know what Sam feels she is lacking, but Sam exits the conversation: "The light changes. She walks away so fast, I can't ask her what she means by that. Can't ask her what it is she needs" (31). This exchange alludes to a larger issue: that Jade is never asked what she needs by adults and caregivers around her, so she is unable to truly fulfill her needs. While Jade has close friends in her neighborhood (notably, Lee Lee), Jade's advantage of being a scholarship student at St. Francis creates a gap in their experience; Jade and Sam also bond over being among the select few in their communities to have the opportunities afforded by attending an elite private school. Jade tells Sam, "I know what it's like to feel kind of guilty for being the one to get what others don't have access to" (57).

Jade's life is full of disappointments, big and small, many of which stem from bad circumstance. This is best exemplified in Chapter 14, when Jade spends her birthday alone after her mother goes to work and both of her closest friends (Lee Lee and Sam) cancel. Jade's father does not come to give Jade the gift that he promised her. In each instance, it was simply bad circumstance—not, by contrast, malicious intent—that prevented Jade's family and closest friends from seeing her. Jade's mother has to work to support the family; Jade's father is portrayed as kindhearted but hapless; Lee Lee was "on punishment" because of a fight with her aunt; Sam was sick.

Another theme introduced in this section is the experience of being the object of philanthropic "do-gooders." Jade is tired of Mrs. Parker constantly reminding her about the various opportunities available to her, and she does not want to be seen as a project or a "problem" that needs solving, which is frequently how Maxine makes her feel. The reader catches a glimpse of this fraught relationship in Chapter 10, when Jade overhears Maxine refer to her as her "mentee." Jade thinks to herself: "*Mentee.* I don't like that word. I just want to be Jade" (42).

A primary motif of *Piecing Me Together* is language, not only in terms of the plot, but also in the way the book is crafted. From the bilingual English/Spanish chapter titles to Jade's comment to her father in Chapter 17 that "language is powerful," language as a motif will help solidify larger themes surrounding self-advocacy and communication. Another motif introduced in this first section is collage art. Jade is a collage artist, and she pieces together scraps from her everyday life—a bus schedule, family photos— to, in her words, "make them beautiful." Underscoring ideas surrounding a fragmented identity, Jade makes art out of different, smaller pieces. Collage art is also a means of communicating for Jade; communication is another primary theme this motif helps to underscore. Beyond the plot, the book is structured such that some chapters are fragmented, one-page statements or vignettes, echoing the feel of a collage.

Chapters 21-40

Chapter 21 Summary: *"mujer a mujer* - woman to woman"

The next Woman to Woman gathering is at the home of
Sabrina, the program's founder. It is "girl talk night" and
tonight's topic is dating: "I can tell by the looks on
everyone's faces who's excited about talking about dating
and who's terrified" (81). Jade is ambivalent about dating;
she does not have much experience and spends most of her
time focusing on school.

The 12 girls and their mentors sit cross-legged on the floor
of Sabrina's lavish home. They go around a circle, and each
of the mentors will offer up a piece of advice she wishes
she had known in high school. One mentor begins by
saying that, in order to love someone else, you must first
love yourself: "All the women are nodding, their heads
moving like synchronized swimmers" (83). Another mentor
reminds the girls that they are still growing and learning
about themselves; their taste in whom they choose to love
will evolve over time "in ways you can't even imagine"
(83). Maxine is noticeably quiet, and Jade wonders if she is
worried about being "called out" for her bad relationship
with Jon, her ex-boyfriend. After the rest of the mentors
have spoken, Sabrina takes out index cards on which the
girls have written questions anonymously. The first
question is "How do I get guys to notice me?" (84). One of
the mentors responds that by "being yourself" (84), the
right person will take notice. When Jade reads the next
question—"How do you get over someone you love?"
(84)—she thinks of how Maxine still has not been able to
move on from Jon.

The session ends with Sabrina making a speech about the girls following their dreams, and how important it is for them to just be themselves. Jade inwardly scoffs: She knows plenty of big dreamers in North Portland, but dreaming alone will not help them overcome the disadvantages of being poor and black. Jade then thinks about how her mother's love "repairs" her when she despairs about her life: "And that's when I believe my dark skin isn't a curse, that my lips and hips, hair and nose don't need fixing. That my dream of being an artist and traveling the world isn't foolish" (85). Jade wonders if there's "a way for a girl like me to feel whole" (86), or if she'll always feel torn apart by other people's expectations of what it means to be a black girl, or a poor girl, or a chubby girl.

Chapter 22 Summary: "*almorzar* - to have lunch"

Jade and Sam walk into school from the bus stop, and Sam asks Jade if she'll be able to hang out with her that weekend. However, Jade is booked all weekend between homework and Woman to Woman: "I feel bad that I don't have any time to hang out with Sam. We only spend time together on the bus or at lunch" (87). Sam jokingly wonders if, due to Jade's busy schedule, she will need to find a "new best friend" (87).

Josiah approaches them and asks if they'd like to get lunch with him and Kennedy that afternoon at Zack's, a local burger place. Though Jade does not usually have the money to eat out at lunch, and she rarely hangs out with Josiah and Kennedy (the wealthy black clique at the school), she says yes: "I say okay, but only because E.J. gave me some money. He does that sometimes after he's deejayed at a big event" (88).

Chapter 23 Summary: *"reír* - to laugh"

Jade and Sam join Josiah, Kennedy, and two of their
friends for lunch at Zack's. Kennedy is rude to the server
when she mistakenly gives Kennedy regular fries rather
than sweet potato fries. They take their food back to school
to eat and, in Jade's words, "the whole ride back she
whines about how she's wasted her calories on something
she doesn't really want" (89). On the car ride, the
conversation turns to Northeast Portland and how awful the
neighborhood is; no one but Jade knows that that is where
Sam lives. Jade thinks: "If they feel that way about Sam's
neighborhood, they must think I live in a wasteland" (90).

When the group gets to school, Jade and Sam take leave,
sitting in the hallway to eat their burgers and fries. Alone,
the girls agree that they will never go to lunch with that
group again, though they will go back to Zack's on their
own—the burgers are delicious.

Chapter 24 Summary: *"tener hambre* - to be hungry"

Jade arrives home after school and finds that her mother
has left her a note saying that she has a doctor's
appointment, along with $20 so that Jade can get herself
something for dinner. Jade decides on Dairy Queen.
Halloween is next weekend, and Jade observes carved
pumpkins and fall leaves on her bus ride to the restaurant.

When Jade arrives, there is a long line for food, and Jade
notices a group of teenage boys sitting nearby: "A group of
boys are sitting at a table, all spread out and loud like they
are eating at home in their living room" (93). While waiting
for her food, she overhears the boys pointing to different
girls in the crowd, polling whether each girl is dateable or
not. Jade is not looking at the boys but she can tell when

they point to her: "I know he is pointing to me, which means they are all looking at me—from behind. Not good. The man at the counter calls my number and gives me my food" (93). One boy says she is a five out of ten and comments that she must "break the scale" (94), referring to her weight. One of the other boys responds that "thick girls are fine," and so his friend goads him into talking to Jade. When Jade rebuffs his advance, the boy calls her "every derogatory name a girl could ever be called" (94). Jade gets on the bus to go home and decides she will make a collage using the paper bag from the Dairy Queen.

Chapter 25 Summary: *"llamar* - to name"

Chapter 25 is another one-page fragment, mimicking a collage that Jade is working on. She places the crown in the center of the piece and, in the background, writes a series of words the boy could have called her instead of the derogatory names, among them "scholar," "artist," and "dreamer" (96).

Chapter 26 Summary: *"el barrio* - the neighborhood"

Sam makes plans to visit Jade at her home after school one day, which surprises Jade since Sam's racist grandmother made such a "fuss," in Jade's words, about her neighborhood being one of the most (supposedly) dangerous in Portland.

Jade meets Sam at the bus stop. They stop at Frank's, a grocery store, to get chicken wings before heading home. There they bump into Lee Lee. She hassles Jade about not being available lately and invites both Jade and Sam to her cousin Andrea's house. At Andrea's, Jade gets caught up with how things are at Northside high school. Lee Lee says she is involved in a DIY poetry club, which is an unofficial gathering of students who meet and share their writing. When the time comes for Sam to go home, Jade and Lee Lee both walk her to the bus stop. Jade remarks that Sam's grandmother is scared of North Portland, to which Lee Lee replies that she is baffled, since Northeast Portland is just as impoverished as their neighborhood. Lee Lee says, "White people are a trip. [...] How you gonna live in a 'hood but be afraid to come to another 'hood?" (103).

Chapter 27 Summary: *"agradecido* - thankful"

It is Thanksgiving, and E.J. and Lee Lee join Jade and her mother for their annual holiday tradition: "We go downtown and volunteer at the Portland Rescue Mission. 'We don't have much, but we have more than a lot of other people,' Mom says" (104). After volunteering, the group heads to Jade's mother's house for dinner. As they eat, the conversation turns to Lee Lee's revolutionary-activist history teacher, Mrs. Phillips, who does not celebrate Thanksgiving because the holiday commemorates when "our nation was stolen from indigenous people" (105).

Jade feels embarrassed for not ever having considered that Thanksgiving was a holiday with colonialist origins. Meanwhile, E.J. and Lee Lee compare the experiences of African Americans and Native Americans in the United States, with E.J. saying that he is grateful to be an American, even though the country has mistreated both communities. The rest of the dinner is somber, as everyone mulls over the discussion, until dessert is brought out. The dessert is a cobbler Jade and Lee Lee made—one of the first times either of them has cooked. Everyone laughs as E.J. takes a bite of the cobbler and makes a face, breaking the tension.

Chapter 28 Summary: *"las diferencias* - differences"

It is the first weekend in December and Maxine is driving
Jade to downtown Portland for the next Woman to Woman
outing: a trip to the Portland Art Museum. Maxine asks
Jade if she has ever been to a museum; Jade senses Maxine
is trying to gauge if Jade knows how to behave in a
museum.

Inside the museum, Jade and Maxine join the rest of the
group. As they enter the first exhibit, Maxine takes a call
from Jon and mouths the words *"I'm so sorry. This is
important"* (109) as she leaves the group. Maxine shoos
Jade to go on without her. Jade continues through the
museum, but she is angry with Maxine: "I can't stop
thinking how rude it was for Maxine to take that phone
call—especially from Jon" (110). When Maxine finally re-
joins the group, the trip is over; Maxine asks Jade what she
thought of the experience. Jade says it was "awesome," but
she is still angry. Maxine and Jade go to a restaurant and
Jade steers the conversation toward the things that are
bothering her—not just over the incident at the museum,
but also the condescending way Maxine sometimes treats
her. Jade asks Maxine, "What did you mean when you said
people in North Portland live in a bubble? I live in North
Portland and I—" (111). Maxine tries to justify her
comment, but what irritates Jade most is that Maxine is
"talking about her friends like show knows them, like she
understands anything about them" (112).

As Maxine goes on talking, her words indicate to Jade that
she still does not see her error. Jade asks Maxine why she
signed up to be a mentor in Woman to Woman, and Maxine
says that she is interested in working with young girls and
women—especially women of color—because she wishes
she had had someone to help her when she was in high

school. Jade asks Maxine, "You think I need someone to talk to?" (114). Maxine responds, "I don't know. Do you?" (114). Jade wants to reply yes, but she fears that will confirm Maxine's stereotyped perception of her—that she is just "some 'hood girl with a bunch of problems she has to come and fix" (114). Jade thinks about how different they are and wonders why Mrs. Parker felt they would be a good match.

Chapter 29 Summary: "*la llorona* - the weeping woman"

Jade rides the bus to downtown Portland with her camera. She takes pictures of everything: "Every corner has a story; ever block asks a question. So many worlds colliding all at once. I document my walk, hiding away in places people can't see me so I'm not obvious" (117). Jade comes upon a mural she has never seen before on the Oregon Historical Society building: "There's a larger-than-life mural of Lewis and Clark, Sacagawea with her baby, and York with Seaman, the dog that accompanied them on the trip" (118). Jade takes photos of this mural, the last one zoomed in closely on York's face.

Chapter 30 Summary: "*feliz navidad* - Merry Christmas"

With Christmas coming soon, Jade, Lee Lee, and Sam gather at Jade's house to make holiday cards. Lee Lee worries about crafting homemade cards because she is unable to draw, but Jade tells her that they'll be doing collages—no need to be able to draw. Lee Lee reminisces about how, in sixth grade when she and Jade attended the same middle school, one of Lee Lee's drawings was so bad that their art teacher refused to display it alongside the other students'. Lee Lee says that her skill is poetry; she then asks Sam what she is good at, and Sam does not have an immediate answer: "Sam stops writing. She thinks—longer than I expect—and says, 'I don't know. Nothing like writing poetry or making art'" (121). Jade says that being a good friend is a talent and that Sam is a wonderful friend. Sam thanks her and tells her that she is a good friend, too.

Chapter 31 Summary: *"víspera de Año Nuevo* - New Year's Eve"

Chapter 31 is another one-page fragment, this one detailing the New Year's resolution that Jade makes to herself in collage form, "in black Sharpie marker on top of a background made out of cut-up scriptures, words from newspaper headlines, and numbers from last year's calendar" (123). Her resolution is to: "Be bold. Be brave. Be beautiful. Be brilliant. Be (your) best" (123).

Chapter 32 Summary: *"hermanas* - sisters"

For the next Woman to Woman outing, Maxine has invited Jade to her apartment, where a few of Maxine's friends will join them. Since Jade expressed her concerns, Maxine has been making more of an effort to be a reliable mentor to Jade.

Upon arrival, Jade notes how exquisitely decorated Maxine's apartment is: "Her living room looks like she bought a whole showroom at a furniture store—everything matching and perfectly in its place" (125). When Maxine's friends join them, they start pressing Maxine for an update on her and Jon. Maxine reveals that Jon had been cheating on her and says she and Jon are certainly getting back together. Given Maxine's history of breaking up and getting back together with Jon (and that he is unemployed, and always asking to borrow Maxine's car or money),

Maxine's friends encourage her to remain broken up: "Kira and Bailey say, almost in unison, 'Just don't take him back'" (127). Jade starts to feel bad for Maxine and changes the conversation to college, asking each of the women what their experience was like. The conversation then turns to sex and dating, and Maxine argues with her friends that Jade is too young to discuss the topic. As they wrap up the evening, one of Maxine's friends tells Jade that if she ever has questions about sex or dating, she should feel free to get in touch with her. Maxine overhears and tells her friend to "leave Jade alone" because "'she is not like that. She's smart [...] She's not going to mess things up by getting caught up with some guy,' she says. 'I'm going to see to it that she doesn't end up like one of *those girls*'" (130). Jade is offended, knowing that Maxine is referring to the girls from Jade's neighborhood.

Chapter 33 Summary: "*lo mismo* - the same"

Jade finishes her first collage about York, Lewis, and Clark. Jade's mother asks her why York fascinates her so much. "[I] tell her that it's interesting to me that a black man made the journey to find this place—the Pacific Northwest—when I all I want to do is leave it" (131). Jade starts working on her next collage, which is also related to this idea of escape: "Tonight I make something about a different expedition. The one I am on. I want to get out, and I feel like a traitor for admitting it" (131). Jade ruminates on Maxine's comment. On the one hand, she is one of "those girls": "I am the Kool-Aid-drinking, fast food-eating unhealthy girl she wants to give nutrition classes to. I know all about food stamps and dollar menus and layaway" (131). On the other hand, Jade is different:

> I am the girl who spends her summers reading books
> and working, tutoring at the rec [...] I am the girl

who knows when to stop talking back to a teacher because I know my mother will be waiting for me when I get home, asking me if I forgot who raised me. I am the girl who dreams of going places: to college, to grad school, all around the world, if I can (132).

Still, there are indisputable ways in which she is "just the same" (132).

Chapter 34 Summary: *"pertenecer* - to belong"

Jade's schedule has been full lately: "Life has only been school all day, tutoring afterward, and sad looks from Sam, who thinks I have forgotten about her" (133). On one of her rare free days, Jade joins Sam at Pioneer Place, the local mall. Jade does not plan on buying anything, but she accompanies Sam just so they can spend time together: "Sam drags me in and out of stores for the rest of the afternoon. The only stores we go into are for skinny girls, so I'm glad I don't have money to buy anything" (133).

At a clothing store, Sam goes off to the dressing room, leaving Jade alone. A salesclerk approaches Jade, and Jade tells her that she is waiting for her friend and plans to browse in the meantime. Jade moves away from the clothes and heads to the jewelry section, and the salesclerk follows her. The salesclerk asks to take Jade's purse because it is "store policy" that all guests have their bags held behind the counter; however, Jade looks around and notices that all the other women in the store—all white women, she notes—are still carrying their purses. Jade points out that not everyone is participating in this store policy and she refuses to give hers up. When the salesclerk threatens to ask her to leave if she does not cooperate, Jade leaves the store voluntarily.

Jade sits on a bench just outside the store, and when Sam comes out, Jade relays the whole incident to her. Sam is in disbelief—however, she does not believe that Jade was forced out of the store because of race-related discrimination: "I don't think it had anything to do with your race or your size. I think maybe she was just trying to do her job. That's all" (137). Jade is not only upset by the salesclerk, she is also upset by the fact that Sam—supposedly her best friend—does not believe her when she says the incident was race-related.

Chapter 35 Summary: *"negro - black"*

Chapter 35 is a one-page, fragmented vignette that describes Jade's latest collage, made up of words and clippings from magazines and entitled "Things That Are Black and Beautiful" (138). Among them are a "starless night sky," onyx, ink, panthers, "Afro Puffs," and then at the end of the list, herself ("me") (138).

Chapter 36 Summary: *"comer - to eat"*

Jade comes home from a half day of school. She starts working on her math homework but soon runs into a problem set that makes her "stuck and frustrated" (140). Jade's mother tries to help but she does not know anything about Algebra II. Jade says that she will ask Maxine to help her, which irritates her mother, who retorts, "Well, excuse me" (140).

Jade compliments her mother's fish fry as they begin to eat dinner. She then asks her mother if she will come to Woman to Woman's upcoming Healthy Eating, Healthy Living seminar, which sends her mother "into a rage" (141). Jade's mother angrily says that she is too busy to attend the seminar; she also says that Woman to Woman has "some nerve," telling her how to cook. Jade's mother says:

> 'You hanging around all those uppity black women who done forgot where they come from. Maxine know she knows about fried fish. I don't know one black person who hasn't been to a fish fry at least once in their life. Where she from?' (142).

Sensing that her mother needs to voice these concerns, Jade lets her continue to talk about her issues with the organization.

Chapter 37 Summary: *"mi madre* - my mother"

Chapter 37 is another one-page fragment that describes Jade's process for her next collage, which is devoted to her mother: "Photocopied pictures of my mother from when she was an infant till now are spread across the table" (143). She assembles "all the best parts" of her mother there on the page, including "the hair of her teen years," "her hands, when she used to paint her nails," and "the smile from her twenty-first birthday" (143).

Chapter 38 Summary: *"vestido* - dress"

Jade and her mother look at their shared dry erase board calendar. Jade's mother asks Jade, with all the upcoming Woman to Woman activities on the calendar, if Jade will be able to keep up with her studies. Jade says yes. The next Friday, Woman to Woman has organized an outing to the symphony. Jade's mother remarks on what an "extravagant" event this trip will be; she also suggests that Jade ask Maxine what she should wear, since people are supposed to "dress up." Jade goes to her bedroom and tries on multiple outfits but "nothing looks right" (145), so she decides to get a new dress with the money she has been saving in case of an emergency.

Chapter 39 Summary: *"música* - music"

At the Woman to Woman outing to the symphony, a volunteer with the Oregon Symphony gives the group a talk backstage. Jade observes the volunteer: "She is white, and the black sweater she is wearing makes her skin look pale and washed-out" (146). The volunteer walks the group to the stage so they can see the audience from the perspective of the musicians; she is talking excitedly about the different sections—strings, woodwind, brass, percussion—of the symphony, and how they all function together to form a whole.

Jade suspects the volunteer is somehow offended that the Woman to Woman group does not seem to share her enthusiasm for classical music. The volunteer says:

'You know, some folks don't think they can relate to this kind of music. [...] Now, I know hip-hop is what you kids are all about these days [...] But did you know that James DePreist was one of the first African American conductors on the world stage?' (147).

Maxine speaks on behalf of the group, with "venom in her voice" (148), and assures the volunteer that they know who this artist is. When the backstage tour is over and the Woman to Woman group is seated, Maxine angrily says to one of the other mentors that the volunteer treated them like "poor black heathens who don't know anything worth knowing" (148). Overhearing this, Jade begins thinking that maybe Maxine and Carla "aren't only offended at that woman's stereotypes, but maybe they are upset at the idea of being put in the same category as me and the other girls"

(149). As the lights go down, Jade reflects on the volunteer's stereotyped impression of the Woman to Woman group, which makes her feel hopeless that some people will "only see what they want to see" (149).

Chapter 40 Summary: *"el río* - the river"

Over the next few weeks, Jade does not spend much time with Sam. There are two reasons for this: "Partly because I usually have something to do after school, but mostly because I don't know how to be around her when I know she doesn't think that salesclerk treated me wrong" (151). Jade does not even think that Sam realizes there is tension between the two of them, and she doubts she can be friends with someone who is so disconnected to what she goes through.

It is the end of the day at school, and Sam needs to stop by Mrs. Parker's office before leaving. Jade waits for her. When Sam emerges from the office, she excitedly reports that she has been selected for the study abroad program at St. Francis, and that the trip this year is to Costa Rica. Jade is inwardly devastated by this news: "When she says this, there is a pain in my chest. A real physical pain" (152). Despite her pain, Jade tries to be happy for Sam and congratulates her. At the bus stop, Sam asks Jade if something is wrong. Jade says no but then snaps when Sam suggests that Jade joins the trip—Jade angrily reminds Sam that students need to be nominated in order to participate, and Mr. Flores nominated Sam but not Jade. They ride in silence for most of the way, but when they get close to Sam's stop, Sam asks if Jade can come over that weekend to spend the night. Jade flatly tells her that she needs to ask her mother.

Chapters 21-40 Analysis

Questions of mentorship—who is meant to be a mentor, what is worthy of being taught—arise in this section. Jade senses that Maxine is an imperfect person: "I wonder how it feels to be here as a person who's supposed to have it all together but has some of the same questions as we do" (84). Jade also starts to sense that the mentors at Woman to Woman look down on the mentees: "Listening to these mentors, I feel like I can prove the negative stereotypes about girls like me wrong. That I can and will do more, be more" (86). Ironically, Jade feels she needs to defeat stereotypes even within Woman to Woman. Jade continues to feel distant from Maxine, sensing their differences keenly: "I don't say anything. I'm just sitting here, thinking how different we [Jade and Maxine] are. How I'm not sure why Mrs. Parker thought we'd be a good pair" (115). However, Maxine does pose an opportunity for Jade to escape her current situation: "Maxine reminds me that I am a girl who needs saving. She knows I want out and she has come with a lifeboat. Except I just don't know if I can trust her hand" (130).

While Woman to Woman provides many opportunities for the mentees (most notably, a college scholarship), elements of the program are problematic. It is challenging (and exhausting) for Jade keep up with the opportunities presented to her by Woman to Woman. She has no time to see her friends. As Sam says when explaining that Lee Lee's poetry club would have been ruined at St. Francis: "No freedom to just be, you know?" (102). There is also the issue that the organization can be condescending to the very people it claims to serve. For instance, Jade's mother feels the Healthy Eating, Healthy Living seminar is an affront to her cooking in Chapter 36, and Jade's mentioning the seminar inspires her mother to unleash her concerns with Woman to Woman:

> Mom won't stop talking. She goes on and on about Maxine and Sabrina and how they are a different type of black, how she knows she's going to get tired of dealing with them for the next two years. 'I swear, if you didn't need that scholarship, I'd take you out of that program. I'm not sending you there to be in no cooking class. What that got to do with getting into college?' (142).

This section also sees the friendship between Jade and Sam deepening: In Chapter 22, Sam refers to Jade as her best friend; in Chapter 30, Jade affirms to Sam that "you're a good friend, too" (122). However, in Chapter 34, Sam's disregard for a racist experience Jade had in the mall threatens the integrity of that friendship: "I don't know what's worse. Being mistreated because of the color of your skin, your size, or having to prove that it really happened" (137).

Chapters 41-60

Chapter 41 Summary: *"familia* - family"

Jade has been distancing herself from Maxine since the symphony outing, but she agrees to attend "Soul Food Sunday," Maxine's weekly family tradition. Maxine and Jade are in charge of bringing dessert to the dinner, so they stop by an expensive pastry shop on their drive to Maxine's family home. Jade observes that they are headed to a wealthy neighborhood: "I can tell we're entering the rich part of Portland. We're driving up a winding road that's got us so high, my ears are popping" (157). They arrive at

Maxine's family home, which has "three garage doors and a balcony that wraps around the front of the house" (158). Maxine's sister, Mia, greets Maxine in the driveway. They head inside, and Maxine introduces Jade to the rest of her family: her parents (Mr. and Mrs. Winters), her brother (Nathan), and his wife (Abby).

While they finish preparations for dinner, Mia and Nathan ask Jade questions: "Mia says to me, 'So tell us about yourself, Jade. You're an artist, right? I'd love to have you stop by my gallery'" (159). Mia is a gallery owner, Maxine explains. Whenever questions are asked of Jade, Maxine answers on Jade's behalf, and Jade senses that Maxine is worried that Jade will respond in the "wrong" way. Midway through the meal, Mrs. Winters says it is time do "check-ins." Everyone goes around the table and announces what is new or noteworthy in their life: Mr. Winters, a realtor, just sold a house in Laurelhurst, and Mia says that work is "amazing" (162) and that she and her husband are doing well. When it is Nathan's turn, he says that he and Abby have a major announcement: Abby is pregnant. Everyone at the table erupts with exclamations of excitement, except for Maxine: "I look at Maxine, who is the only one not smiling. She rakes her yams from one side of the plate to the other, never taking a bite" (163). Given Nathan's big news, the check-ins stop and Maxine does not provide an update on her life.

When the dinner ends, Mrs. Winters wraps leftovers for Jade to take home. She also offers leftovers to Maxine, offending her. Mrs. Winters explains that while what Maxine is doing with Jade and Woman to Woman is "nice" (165), Maxine does not have a real job, and Mrs. Winters is worried her. Maxine and Mrs. Winters begin to argue. Maxine says that she had hoped that, by bringing Jade to dinner that evening, Mrs. Winters would see that the work

Maxine is doing is important. Mrs. Winters retorts, "I don't care about her sob story, Max. I understand that program is important to you, but you need a real job" (165). Overhearing this, Jade is deeply hurt:

> I want to leave. Just want to go back to my mother
> and eat the food at her table that has no rules about
> the way to use forks and napkins. Want to go where I
> don't have to pretend I'm not hungry, want to go eat
> all this on my plate and not feel greedy (165).

Maxine senses on the car ride home that Jade is upset and asks her what is wrong. Jade says she does not want to talk, and they ride home in silence.

Chapter 42 Summary: "*saber* - to know"

Jade's mother intuitively knows that something is wrong between Jade and Maxine. As they eat the leftovers from Soul Food Sunday, Jade confides that she wants to quit the program because it makes her feel like a "charity case" (168). This angers Jade's mother, who forbids her from quitting. She reminds Jade that she cannot afford to forfeit the college scholarship she will be awarded if she completes the program, also, she does not want Jade to be the sort of person who "walks away" from commitments. Moreover, even if Maxine is "imperfect," Jade can still learn from Maxine:

> 'So what, Maxine isn't perfect? This girl graduated
> from St. Francis as valedictorian. She learned how to
> navigate this white world, and she's trying to show
> you how to do the same. You telling me she has
> nothing to teach you? You better learn how to get
> from this opportunity what you can and let the rest
> fall off your back' (169).

She concludes by saying that Jade needs to "figure it out" (169) and that under no circumstances is Jade quitting the program.

Chapter 43 Summary: *"tener dolor* - to have pain"

Chapter 43 is a one-page, fragmented retelling of a moment from Jade's life. Indirectly, it portrays her sadness and internal struggles related to Maxine and Sam through a scene from Mr. Flores's Spanish class, where they are learning words and phrases related to going to the doctor. Jade observes that "Mr. Flores is always teaching about one kind of thing while I'm thinking about another" (170). The class learns the following phrases: *"No me siento bien.* I don't feel well" and *"Me duele aqúi.* It hurts here" (170).

Chapter 44 Summary: *"hablar* - to speak"

Jade skips the next two Woman to Woman outings, as she is still avoiding Maxine. Even though she misses going places she might not have otherwise gone, Jade does not miss "the lectures about how to eat, how to not be who I am" (171). Jade is at home in bed when she hears a knock at the door. It is Lee Lee, who has come to visit Jade after Jade's mother told her that she needed someone to talk to. Lee Lee insists that Jade confide in her, and Jade admits that she is considering quitting Woman to Woman. Jade says she does not feel she is getting anything out of the program, but Lee Lee agrees with Jade's mother: Jade should not quit the program. Instead, Lee Lee suggests that she speak to whoever is in charge and let them know what she needs, and what needs to change about the program.

Chapter 45 Summary: "*la verdad* - the truth"

Jade calls Maxine the following day and asks if they can
get together. Maxine agrees right away, and she goes to
Jade's house. When Maxine hugs Jade as a greeting, Jade
can tell she feels guilty: "She holds on to me as if to say,
I'm sorry for hurting you" (174). They drive to a restaurant
for dinner. Fortified by her conversation with Lee Lee, Jade
starts voicing her concerns on the drive there:

> 'I want something more from Woman to Woman [...]
> I don't want to sound ungrateful. I mean, I do like
> going on all those trips, but sometimes you make me
> feel like you come to fix me; only, I don't feel
> broken. Not until I'm around you' (176).

Maxine apologies for hurting Jade and for not allowing her
to speak for herself. She then asks what Woman to Woman
can do better. Jade says she would like to learn about "real-
life things" (177), like how to create a budget; she would
love an outing to Maxine's sister's gallery, and to learn
about how Mia started her business as a gallery owner.
When Maxine asks if there is anything else, Jade brings up
Jon—but Maxine stops her. She tells Jade she is right, and
then suggests they talk about him over dinner.

Chapter 46 Summary: "*abandoner* - to quit"

Jade and Maxine wait to be seated at the restaurant.
Conversation between them flows more easily now that
Jade has cleared the air. When they are at the table, the
conversation turns to Jon. Jade clarifies that she is not
"anti-Jon," she is "pro-Maxine" (180). Maxine begins to
cry and says, "Oh, Jade, you have me in here, getting all
emotional. You're not supposed to be giving me the
advice" (180). Maxine agrees that she needs to end things

for good with Jon. Maxine offers to strike a deal with Jade: She will quit Jon, and Jade will not quit the program. Jade agrees: "Deal" (180).

Chapter 47 Summary: "*orar* - to pray"

Jade is running late for school, and she grabs two Pop-Tarts as she leaves. As she approaches the front door, E.J. asks her from his bed in the living room if Jade has heard what happened Saturday night. E.J. tells her that a 15-year-old black teen by the name of Natasha Ramsey was manhandled by the police at a house party. Natasha has fractured ribs and a broken jaw and is in the hospital in critical condition. Jade leaves for school, disturbed by the news: "I go to class and the entire time all I can think about is Natasha Ramsey. Her smiling face" (183).

Chapter 48 Summary: "*fantasma* - ghost"

At lunchtime, Jade is still thinking about Natasha Ramsey, but no one at the school is talking about the news:

> All day long I've been whispering prayers. Natasha's name haunts me. No one speaks her name or mentions what happened. It's as if no one in the school knows or cares that an unarmed black girl was assaulted by the police just across the river (184).

Jade is deep in thought in the lunch line when she realizes that the lunch lady, Ms. Weber, is telling her to "keep the line moving" (185). Ms. Weber also tells Hannah, one of Jade's white classmates, to keep moving. Hannah rolls her eyes and suggests Ms. Weber might be PMS-ing. When Jade laughs, Ms. Weber sends her to Mrs. Parker's office because of her "attitude problem" (185).

Jade stands against the wall outside of Mrs. Parker's office while Ms. Weber gives her side of the story. After she is finished, Jade enters Mrs. Parker's office and explains that even though Hannah was the one being disrespectful, Jade is somehow getting the punishment. Mrs. Parker does not admit that Ms. Weber was lying about how Jade behaved in the lunchroom; instead, Mrs. Parker glosses over Ms. Weber's behavior and simply says that she is trying to help Jade. She suggests that Jade go home to collect herself so they can start fresh the next day and move on from the misunderstanding.

Chapter 49 Summary: *"el teléfono* - the telephone"

Sam calls Jade and asks if she is okay after the incident in the lunchroom. Sam says that she is shocked they sent Jade home, but then again, Jade was "mouthing off" (189). Jade points out that Hannah was the one "mouthing off" to Ms. Weber, but she can get away with it because she is white. Sam disagrees, saying that Hannah is able to get away with it because she is rich. Jade responds by saying that that is what people will say about Natasha Ramsey—that her being black had nothing to do with her brutal beating by the police. Sam says "who?" at the mention of Natasha Ramsey because she has not heard about the incident. There is silence between Jade and Sam, and they hang up.

Chapter 50 Summary: *"respirar* - to breathe"

After hanging up with Sam, Jade calls Lee Lee and asks if she heard the news about Natasha Ramsey. Like Jade, Lee Lee says that she has been thinking about it all day. Unlike St. Francis, Lee Lee's school had a town hall meeting for students who needed to talk about what happened. Lee Lee says that one of her teachers gave them an assignment to write a poem about any victim of police brutality, but that does not feel sufficient to Lee Lee and she begins to cry. She confides to Jade, who immediately agrees, that the incident just feels "too close" (192), as if either one of them could have been the victim.

Chapter 51 Summary: "*borrar* - to erase"

That night, Jade cannot sleep. Just before dawn, she starts another collage about York. Jade thinks about how Clark wrote that some of the tribes had never seen a black person before. The tribes "thought York was magic, thought he was some kind of supernatural being. York would tell them he was a black man, nothing had happened to his skin" (194). Jade ruminates on what York must have felt when they said things like that to him: "Did he remember existing in a world where no one thought him strange, thought him beast? Did he remember being human?" (194).

Chapter 52 Summary: "*perseverar* - to persevere"

Jade and Maxine go for a walk through Columbia Park, and Jade talks about her problems with Sam. Maxine's advice to Jade is to say something to Sam about how her actions and words make Jade feel. Jade notes this is another area of her life that she can improve if she makes her voice heard: "Something else I need to speak up about" (196). Jade feels strengthened after her conversation with Maxine; she is not ready to "quit" on herself, her friendship with Sam, and her dreams.

Chapter 53 Summary: "*para abogar* - to advocate"

Jade walks into Mr. Flores's classroom as he is eating lunch and watching a news clip about Natasha Ramsey on his laptop. Jade joins him to watch the news report, in which a doctor says that physically Natasha will recover.

Mr. Flores says he is glad that Natasha will be okay but wonders what the psychological damage will be.

When Mr. Flores asks Jade what brings her to his classroom, Jade tells him that she wants to know why he did not nominate her for the study abroad program. Jade lays out all the reasons she deserved to go:

> 'I have an A in your class. You always pick me to help people in the class who are struggling. And, you know this is an opportunity to do volunteer work in and service and that would look really good on my college resume; plus, without the study abroad program, I doubt I'll ever, ever get an opportunity to travel internationally' (198).

Mr. Flores's face flushes with color, and he explains that while Jade deserved to go, he wanted to be fair to his other students, who also deserve opportunities. Jade explains that she does not think the other students were undeserving, but she wishes she could be seen as "someone who can give" instead of solely as "someone who needs" (199). Mr. Flores does not answer Jade's question and instead reaffirms that he needed to be fair to the other students. Jade thanks Mr. Flores for his time before going to the bathroom, where she hides in a stall and cries.

Chapter 54 Summary: "*la primavera* - spring"

It is the weekend before spring break, and Jade sits in the living room with Sam's grandfather while Sam is in the attic, trying to find a suitcase. Jade had promised to sit with Sam while she packs for her trip to Costa Rica. She is doing her best to control her feelings about not being nominated: "I am really trying to be mature and not take my disappointment out on Sam" (203). Jade asks what is on the itinerary for the trip, and Sam replies that she will mostly do volunteer work with school children and help their teachers. Sam tries her best to downplay the trip, but Jade notes that she is "not a good actress" (203). Sam eventually asks Jade if she is mad that Sam is going to Costa Rica; Jade replies no—she is mad because she is not going. Sam says that it is not fair for Jade to be jealous, since Jade is the one who gets to do "cool things all the time" (203). Furthermore, she has always been supportive of Jade, so why is it that Jade cannot be happy for Sam "just this once" (205). Jade replies that SAT prep and tutoring after school are not the same as a trip to Costa Rica; Sam knows nothing about only being included in programs that want to "*fix* you." Still upset, Jade tells Sam to have fun on her trip and leaves.

Chapter 55 Summary: "*miedo* - fear"

Jade has an entire week off for spring break, and she spends her time hanging out with Lee Lee and Lee Lee's cousin Andrea. The girls chat about dating, Lee Lee's ex, and a boy named Tyrell who has a crush on Andrea. The girls walk to Columbia Park and Jade takes pictures: "We keep walking. The whole way, I'm documenting the city, taking photos of strangers I've never seen, strangers I see every day. Like the woman who is always sitting on her porch, knitting something" (208). As the girls continue to walk, they see a police car with its lights flashing in the distance: "White cops have pulled over a black woman. We walk closer. Stop at enough distance not to be noticed but close enough to be witnesses" (209). The girls try to stay calm, but each of them is having a nervous reaction: Lee Lee's hand shakes, Andrea's breathing gets heavier. When the police write the woman a ticket and release her, the girls breathe a sigh of relief. Jade takes Lee Lee's hand and gives it a reassuring squeeze; she reminds them that they are okay, and that the woman is fine.

Chapter 56 Summary: *"liberar* - to release"

Jade prints the photos she took that day. When she starts making her next collage, she is startled by how it unleashes a flood of emotions, all related to racial injustice:

> Every tear I've been holding in goes onto the page. Tears for Mom's swollen ankles after a long day of work, for her jar of pennies. [...] Tears for what happened with Mrs. Weber, the lady at the mall, the boys at Dairy Queen. [...] Tears for every name of unarmed black men and women I know of who've been assaulted or murdered by the police are inked on the page (211).

Chapter 57 Summary: *"silencio* - silence"

When spring break ends, Jade knows that Sam has returned from Costa Rica, but for some reason Sam does not ride the bus to school that day: "Not having Sam's company makes the ride seem longer" (213). When Jade arrives at school, she sees Sam in the hallway and they wave at each other from a distance without smiling.

Chapter 58 Summary: *"pieza por pieza* - piece by piece"

Jade and Maxine go to the Esplanade along the Willamette River; Maxine asks what has been on Jade's mind lately. Jade tells her that she feels as if she keeps being "stitched together and coming undone" (214). Maxine says that she can relate to that feeling and that she often felt that way at St. Francis. They bond over how, as some of the few black students at St. Francis, they often had certain things assumed about them—Maxine admits that her fellow students often assumed she was on scholarship. They agree that it is "exhausting" to have to combat people's expectations and assumptions of them simply because of their race.

Maxine also goes into more detail about how race-related assumptions had an effect on her upper-middle-class upbringing. For example, Maxine's father, a real estate agent, would always advise his black clients to remove any African American artwork and photos from their homes in order to have greater odds of selling their house. Maxine says that this made her feel conflicted about her blackness. Maxine says, "I guess it made me feel like blackness needed to be hidden, toned down, and that whiteness was good, more acceptable" (216). Jade assumed Maxine had no idea about her struggles related to race, but now she sees Maxine differently. Maxine is reminded of what her grandmother used to say about the importance of talking it out—"bearing witness," as her grandmother called it: "I think what my grandmother was saying is that it feels good to know someone knows your story, that someone took you in […] She'd tell me, it's how we heal" (218).

Chapter 59 Summary: *"escubar* - to listen"

The next time Jade sees Maxine, Woman to Woman is holding its inaugural Money Matters workshop. Due to Jade's suggestion, not only is Woman to Woman having a workshop on a more practical topic, but it is holding the event at a location within the community it is meant to serve: "We're having the meeting at a small church not too far away from my house. The pastor is letting us use the space. I love that I didn't even need to take a bus or get a ride from Maxine to get here" (219). Sabrina, the founder of Woman to Woman, thanks Jade for suggesting this topic and introduces the panelists who will discuss the best ways to make and manage money in college. Jade takes copious notes, which she wants to pass on to her mother, E.J., and Lee Lee: "Bring back something other than food this time" (220).

Chapter 60 Summary: *"anticiparse* - to anticipate"

Chapter 60 is a one-page chapter about Jade's usual routine of posting her weekly schedule to the dry erase calendar she and her mother keep on the fridge. Jade puts a "big circle" around the third Saturday of the month, which is when Woman to Woman will visit Maxine's sister's art gallery. Jade is excited for this outing, so much so that she counts the very hours until the outing: "Three more weeks. Twenty-one days. Five hundred and four hours" (221).

Chapters 41-60 Analysis

The problems between Jade and Maxine escalate in this section. When Maxine has Jade over to her family home for dinner in Chapter 41, she literally silences Jade: "Maxine is acting like she's afraid that if I open my mouth, I'll say the wrong thing, embarrass her or something. She seems nervous" (160). Jade overhears Maxine tell her mother that her primary motivation for joining Woman to Woman was to prove to her family that she was doing something good with her life. However, Mrs. Winters (Maxine's mother) explicitly says that she does not care about Jade's "sob story"—at the end of the day, her priority is Maxine and making sure that she can support herself financially. The implication is that Maxine's work with Woman to Woman does not give Maxine full financial independence, and Mrs. Winters does not consider Maxine's mentoring work as a "real" job (165). Following the dinner, Jade feels used by Maxine. The experience makes her question her involvement with the group. Jade seriously considers quitting:

> I wanted to be in Woman to Woman because I thought I'd actually learn something about being a woman. About how to be a successful woman. So far all I've learned is how to make sure there are low-fat, vegan-friendly snacks at girl talk sessions. It's got me thinking, is that all mentorship is? Taking someone younger than you to places they can't afford? (173).

The major turning point, in terms of Jade's personal evolution, occurs when Jade decides to speak up for herself: "I need to speak up for myself. For what I need, for what I want" (174). Jade starts in Chapter 45, when she tells Maxine that she needs Maxine to start showing up to events, and she needs Woman to Woman to start listening to the needs of the mentees. In Chapter 53, Jade tells Mr. Flores that she deserves to be nominated for the study abroad program. In Chapter 70, Jade tells Sam exactly why it offends her when Sam disregards Jade's feelings and essentially claims that the racism she experiences is not real. Once Jade begins to make her voice heard, both her transformation and the transformation of Woman to Woman begin to accelerate. Chapter 60 signals one of the first events sponsored by Woman to Woman that will address the needs and wants of its members; it is an outing to Maxine's sister's art gallery, which has Jade truly excited, underscoring Jade's passion for art.

Chapters 61-76

Chapter 61 Summary: *"las manos* - hands"

E.J. has a gig deejaying for a new restaurant on Thursdays and Fridays, so Jade has the house to herself when Maxine calls and asks what Jade is doing. Jade says that she is just waiting for her mother to come home from work to help take out her braids so that they can redo them. Maxine offers to come over to help do her hair, and Jade calls her mother at work and asks if that is okay. Jade's mother says it is fine.

Maxine arrives and they start the process of taking down Maxine's hair. When Maxine's mother arrives home, she starts making dinner for the three of them. Since Maxine is admittedly "only good at salads," Jade's mother offers to help teach her some of the basics of cooking as she prepares dinner. Meanwhile, Jade sits at the kitchen table practicing her Spanish. She purposely recites words that relate to cooking: "To Peel—Pelar. To Cut—Cortar. To Chop—Picar" (225). Jade, Jade's mother, and Maxine all participate in an exchange of knowledge: "I get Mom to try a few words. And while I am teaching Mom, she is teaching Maxine what a pinch of that and a dab of this means" (225).

Chapter 62 Summary: *"practicar* - to practice"

The day Jade has been waiting for—the Woman to Woman event at Mia's art gallery—has finally arrived. Maxine drives Jade to the art gallery and they arrive just in time for the opening remarks by Woman to Woman's founder. She introduces Mia along with the other black entrepreneur speakers on the panel. Mia takes the stage and says she thinks of her gallery as the "people's gallery," meaning she curates "work that speaks to current issues, that is made by artists from marginalized groups" (227).

Jade looks around the gallery: "We are surrounded by life-size portraits of black women. They look like if you walk up to the paintings and say hello, they will say hi back to you. They look like regal queens but also like my next-door neighbors" (227). Up close, Jade takes in every detail of each portrait; the images of black women remind her of herself, her mother, and her friends. Jade tells Maxine that this trip to the art gallery is one of the best events Woman to Woman has ever had, and then she asks if Mia ever offers internships. Maxine says yes and suggests that Jade ask Mia directly. When Jade does, Mia says that she offers two paid internships jobs at the gallery and she thinks Jade would be a great fit for the role. Mia also says that she would love to see more of Jade's collage work. The event concludes with Mia having everyone close their eyes and reflecting silently on what they learned at the art gallery.

Chapter 63 Summary: "*soledad* - loneliness"

Chapter 63 is another one-page fragment, consisting of Jade's thoughts on the dissolution of her friendship with Sam. Jade jots notes on "How I Know Sam's Not My Friend Anymore" (231). Sam no longer exchanges looks with Jade in Mr. Flores's class: "Even when something is funny, she doesn't turn to me and laugh. She'd rather hold it in, keep her joy to herself" (231).

Chapter 64 Summary: "*oportunidad* - opportunity"

Woman to Woman has its second Money Matters workshop, again held at a local community church in Jade's neighborhood. After the event, the founder of Woman to Woman approaches Jade and asks her if she has a piece she would like to contribute to the art auction at their annual fundraiser. Jade excitedly tells her yes, of course—she would love to give them one of her collages.

Maxine walks Jade home, and Jade tells her mother that she will be donating one of her collages to the auction. Jade's mother worries that Jade may be taken advantage of—that she will not get anything in return. Jade explains that she will get is exposure within the art community, but she also likes being able to give back to the organization that is helping her: "I like being able to say I'm not just getting an opportunity from Woman to Woman, but that I am helping to keep it thriving. Don't you think that's a good thing?" (233). Jade's mother agrees, but she wants to make sure this is really something Jade wants to do; Jade's mother also worries that, because the art auction is such a fancy event, Jade will feel out of place, as if she is being ogled like "a zoo animal all night" (233). Maxine reassures Jade's mother that she will not let that happen. Jade asks Maxine if she will need to make a speech at the event; Maxine says no, but she should be prepared to talk to guests and have a few talking points about her art, her education, and her life goals.

Chapter 65 Summary: "*confianza* - confidence"

Jade is dressed up and feels confident as she and Maxine get ready for the art auction: "Other than these heels Maxine suggested I buy, I am feeling good" (236).

When they arrive at the event, Jade is pleased to realize that she is not as nervous as she thought she would be—the preparing she did with Maxine pays off. Jade feels like "some kind of celebrity" (237) with all the guests approaching her to ask if she is the young lady who made the collages. One of the board members of Woman to Woman tells Jade that she loves her work and that she would love to hear what her plans are for college. When a couple asks Jade what is the best part of Woman to Woman, Jade answers that the organization "really listens" to the concerns of the mentees.

At the end of the evening, Jade is approached by the winner of the auction: "He is a tall brown man with a watch on his wrist that says he could buy all of the art at this auction and not miss a dime" (238). He shakes Maxine's hand and says he has his eye on her and is very taken with her work. He asks her what she is working on, and Jade responds by saying: "Right now I am working on a series of collages about police brutality against unarmed black women and men" (240). The man says that the "world is in for a big awakening" once Jade's art is more widely known. When the conversation ends, Jade reflects on how wonderful it was to display her art publicly at this event, and how she is feeling both seen and heard.

Chapter 66 Summary: *"la tarea* - homework"

The following day, Jade and Lee Lee do their homework together at Jade's house. Lee Lee is working on an essay about media use in social movements, an assignment that Jade finds fascinating. When they finish their homework, Lee Lee offers to recite the poem she wrote for Natasha Ramsey in one of her classes. Jade is impressed by the poem, saying that she wants to "do something with it" (242). It seems like a waste for the poem—not just Lee Lee's, but the work of her entire class—not to be shared with a wider audience:

> For the rest of the night we think up a plan to have an open mic and art show in honor of Natasha Ramsey. We get so caught up with our idea that we plan every detail. Lee Lee will be the MC […] I'll have some of my art on display […] I'll ask Josiah if he'll be our social media person and help us promote it (242).

They want to have the event at Mia's art gallery: "I sure hope she meant it when she said her gallery was for the people" (243).

Chapter 67 Summary: *"renacimiento* - rebirth"

Chapter 67 is another one-page fragment that describes the collage that Jade is working on for the upcoming art show: "I've been combining moments from different photos, blending decades, people and words that don't belong together. Knitting history into the beautiful, bloody tapestry it is" (244). In this collage, she takes pictures of recent victims of racist police brutality (Trayvon Martin and Michael Brown) and juxtaposes them with victims from earlier in United States history (Emmett Till). She depicts modern-day figures conversing with historical figures—"Rosa Parks and Sandra Bland talk with each other under southern trees. Coretta Scott King is holding Aiyana Mo'Nay Stanley-Jones in her arms"—and, in doing so, she "rewrite[s] history" (244).

Chapter 68 Summary: *"legado* - legacy"

Breaking from the narrative of Jade's life, Chapter 68 is Jade's historical imagining of Lewis and Clark's journey with a focus on York's involvement:

> 1805. Lewis and the rest of the explorers reached the Pacific Ocean in November. [...] After all those days searching for the Missouri River, after being trusted to carry a gun, after being listened to, after having some kind of say, York return to St. Louis with the others. The others were welcomed back as national heroes. [...] But York? He didn't get anything (245).

Jade wonders if maybe York was fine without getting land, so long as he got his freedom: "All York wanted was to hold on to that feeling, that feeling when you stand at the ocean, letting the water brush up to your feet and run away again" (246). In 1816, York was eventually freed from slavery, but even with his freedom, Jade notes that York had nothing to pass on to his children. She connects York's having nothing to give with the present: "And isn't this what the man in the Money Matters workshop was telling us when he was explaining how it is that some are rich and some are poor?" (246).

Chapter 69 Summary: "*trabajar* - to work"

Chapter 69 is a one-page fragment that reveals that Mia is enthusiastic about the idea of a community art show for Natasha Ramsey and agrees to host it at her gallery. The chapter also describes the whirlwind of work going into preparing for the event: "Mia was so excited about our idea that she decided to call up a few of her friends, and now we have three professional artists who've donated their work for the event" (247). Local high school students will also contribute art for the show. Lee Lee is working on a new poem, while Jade works on her collage: "The only noise in the kitchen is her pen on the page crossing out and adding in, writing and rewriting stanzas, mixed with the slicing of scissors, the tearing of paper. On and on we go until the sun meets the moon" (247).

Chapter 70 Summary: "*arreglar* - to fix"

In Spanish class, Mr. Flores pairs Jade and Sam together for partner work. Their assignment is to improvise a conversation in Spanish based on words written on flashcards. Sam seems nervous: "Sam bites her lip and picks up the card that's on top" (248). Sam begins, practicing the basic conversational skills according to the cards: "Jade, qué vas a hacer esta noche?" (248). When it is Jade's turn to initiate the conversation, she uses her own words and begins by saying "Lo siento," to which Sam replies, "Yo también" (249). Jade says that Maxine advised her not to give up on people; Sam says that her grandfather says that she has a lot to learn and that she needs to learn to listen more. Sam admits that she is uncomfortable talking to Jade about race because she feels powerless to do anything to fix the situation. Jade tells her that it is not about needing to do anything but just about her listening to Jade's feelings: "When you brush it off like I'm making it up or blowing things out of proportion, it makes me feel like my feelings don't matter to you" (249).

Chapter 71 Summary: *"redimir* - to redeem"

At the end of Spanish class, Mr. Flores calls Jade to his desk. When the rest of the students have emptied into the hallway, Mr. Flores says how proud he is of her for all that she is doing for Natasha Ramsey. Mr. Flores plans to attend the art show, and he even intends to give extra credit to any student who attends. Then, Mr. Flores closes the classroom door. He tells her he wanted to speak about the study abroad program. He apologizes to her: "I've been thinking about what you said. And I wanted to let you know I am so sorry I overlooked you" (251). Mr. Flores then reveals that he spoke with Mrs. Parker, and so long as Jade keeps her grades up, they have reserved her a spot in the program for next year. Jade thanks him, but he tells her there is no need to thank him—Jade earned this.

Chapter 72 Summary: *"perdón* - forgiveness"

Hearkening back to Chapter 63, in which Sam ruminates on "How I Know Sam Isn't My Friend Anymore," Chapter 72 is a one-page fragment with Jade's thoughts on her reconciliation with Sam. Jade jots notes on "How I Know Sam Is My Friend" (251). There are mundane indicators ("We ride the bus to and from school together"), but also Jade determines that the central problem that drove them apart has been resolved: "When we misunderstand each other, we listen again. And again" (253).

Chapter 73 Summary: *"microfono abierto* - open mic"

Jade, Lee Lee, and Sam all sit together at the kitchen table in Jade's house. The three of them are working out a plan for the art gallery event for Natasha Ramsey: E.J. is going to deejay, Mia will manage any art purchases, Maxine and Mia will be responsible for promoting the event, Josiah will set up a livestream for people who are not able to attend, and Sam will be a greeter.

Sam wonders if there is anything else she can contribute, and Lee Lee suggests that they print out poems that Sam, or anyone else who would like to take the mic, can read aloud. Same chooses a poem to read by Martin Espada titled "How We Could Have Lived or Died This Way" (255).

Chapter 74 Summary: *"la gente* - the people"

The night of the event for Natasha Ramsey has arrived: "The gallery is full of family, friends, and community members. Everyone from Woman to Woman is here because Sabrina made this an official monthly outing" (256). Jade does not realize the full extent of the crowd until she stands at the front of the stage and looks out, seeing her mother and father, along with Mrs. Parker from St. Francis; even the parents of Natasha Ramsey are in attendance. Jade takes a picture of the crowd: "This one, I

will not rip or reconfigure. This one, I will leave whole"
(257).

Chapter 75 Summary: *"poema* - poem"

Chapter 75 reproduces Lee Lee's poem, which is titled
"Black Girls Rising" (258). The poem is a call to other
black girls for freedom and empowerment. The poem
begins with "Our black bodies, sacred. / Our black bodies,
holy" (258). The body of the poem alludes to the violence
that threatens black girls on a daily basis:

> This black girl tapestry, this black body / that gets
> dragged out of school desks, slammed onto linoleum
> floor, / tossed about at pool side, pulled over and
> pushed onto grass, / arrested never to return home, /
> shot on doorsteps, on sofas while sleeping / and
> dreaming of our next day (259).

It ends with "Our bodies so black, so beautiful. / Here, still.
/ Rising. / Rising" (259).

Chapter 76 Summary: *"libertad* - freedom"

The final chapter of the book contains more of Jade's
reflections on York: "In 1832 Clark reported that York was
on his way back to St. Louis to be reunited with him"
(260). Clark claimed that York was not happy with his
freedom and wanted to go back to work for Clark—but
Jade does not believe that story.

Instead of York returning to Clark, Jade imagines York
traveling west:

> I see him crossing rivers, crossing mountains, seeing
> Native Americans who were so awed by him. This

time he is no one's servant or slave. This time he tells them the whole story, tells how he is the first of his kind. This time he speaks for himself (261).

Jade imagines herself traveling alongside York, both of them free and black, "discovering what we are really capable of" (261).

Chapters 61-76 Analysis

In the concluding chapters of *Piecing Me Together,* Sam learns to advocate for herself and finds freedom in artistic expression. Woman to Woman evolves alongside Jade as she learns what she needs.

Chapter 61 offers up a vision of perfect mentorship—one in which everyone has something to learn and something to teach. The chapter begins with Jade being concerned that Maxine will judge her mother's house for its imperfections:

> I get anxious about the things she'll see that maybe she hasn't noticed before, like how the dining room table isn't a real dining room table and how none of the furniture matches, or how there's a crack in the ceiling, chipped paint on some of the walls (223).

This is the first time that Maxine has ever stayed for an extended period in Jade's family home. In this chapter, Maxine's bonding with Jade reaches a deeper level: She helps Jade with her hair and she joins the family for dinner, made by Jade's mother. All the while, Jade's mother offers Maxine advice about "life and love" (225). This chapter marks a turning point in Jade and Maxine's relationship, when Maxine stops seeing Jade as an object of pity and starts practicing a truer, more authentic form of mentorship. Contrasted with Chapter 41, in which Maxine tries to control how Jade presents herself, she now advises Jade to "just be herself" (235).

In this section, Watson further develops the historical figure of York as a symbol of black freedom and personal exploration. In fact, the novel concludes with a historical re-imagining by Jade that places her right alongside him as they find freedom. Jade addresses York directly in Chapter 68:

> Clark eventually gave you work and his freedom. I wonder what it would have been like if York had received that land and that money, and his freedom. What would he have built? Would he have left it to his children? […] And isn't this what the man in the Money Matters workshop was telling us when he was explaining how it is that some are rich and some are poor? Isn't that how it works? You pass on what you were given (246).

Jade imagines how York felt when he was so close to freedom: "That feeling of looking out and not being able to see an end or beginning. That feeling that reminds you how massive this world is, how tiny the powerful humans are" (246). Like York, knowing what she knows from Woman to Woman and her experiences at St. Francis, Jade can see what real freedom and real power look like—and yet, also like York, she does not have or control that freedom. In the concluding chapter of the novel, Jade imagines herself alongside York, both of them holding maps and "discovering" what they are "really capable of" (261).

Jade Butler

Jade Butler is the protagonist of *Piecing Me Together* and the book is written from her perspective. Jade is a young, black girl from North Portland, a socioeconomically disadvantaged area of the city. Jade is a junior at St. Francis, an elite (mostly white) private school, having been awarded a scholarship to attend. As a scholarship student, Jade is often presented with "opportunities" by school administrators to improve her lot in life: "But girls like me, with coal skin and hula-hoop hips, whose mommas barely make enough money to keep food in the house, have to take opportunities every chance we get" (7). Jade lives with her mother, who works two jobs, as well as her uncle E.J., a semi-employed deejay who dropped out of college.

As a poor, black, heavyset female, Jade's identity is made up of multiple categories that subject her to cultural discrimination: "Something happens when people tell me I have a pretty face, ignoring me from the neck down. When I watch the news and see unarmed black men and women shot dead over and over, it's kind of hard to believe this world is mine" (85). Jade's evolution in the book revolves around her learning to be her own advocate.

Maxine Winters

Maxine is Jade's mentor in the organization Woman to Woman. She is an upper-middle-class black woman and a St. Francis alum. Jade and Maxine's relationship gets off to a rough start when Maxine stands Jade up at her first-ever Woman to Woman meeting. Jade sees Maxine for the first time when Maxine comes to Jade's family home after missing the meeting. Jade observes her standing on their family doorstep: "She's way too pretty to be here for E.J. Her hair is crinkled and wild, all over the place—but on purpose. She's somewhere in the middle of thick and big-boned. I want to look like that. Instead I'm just plump" (39). At the beginning of the novel, Maxine treats Jade as someone to be fixed, and whose fixing will edify Maxine. By the end of the novel, Maxine has seen how she has been mistreating Jade. Chief among the changes that she makes, Maxine begins listening to Jade, trying to hear what she really needs.

Sam Franklin

Sam Franklin is one of Jade's best friends at St. Francis. She is white with dark brown hair that she usually wears pulled back into a "mess of a ponytail" (11). Sam is from Northeast Portland, an impoverished and almost completely white neighborhood in the city. She is one of the only other scholarship students aside from Jade; they bond over the experience of being from poor families at a school where their peers are incredibly wealthy. Jade meets Sam because they both take the 35 bus to school. Sam has trouble seeing racial bias in everyday life, even when Jade points out how racist incidents affect her. Sam and Jade stop speaking to one another for a period, but once Sam learns to listen to Jade's feelings about the race-related discrimination she faces, their friendship is repaired.

Jade's Mother

Jade's mother is divorced and works two jobs to support her family. Jade is her only child, but her younger brother, E.J., also lives with them in their small house in North Portland. Jade's mother is perpetually tired and under stress: "And though she is resting, I can tell by her face that there is no peace for her, not even in her dreams" (21).

When Jade wants to quit Woman to Woman, her mother forbids it, advising Jade that even imperfect people like Maxine have something to teach her. Jade and her mother have a close relationship: "Mom looks at me with her knowing eyes. She can tell I'm upset. She always knows how I'm feeling, even when I don't know how to put it in words" (35).

E.J. Butler

E.J. is Jade's uncle and her mother's younger brother. He is 20 years old and a college drop-out. He dropped out after a traumatic incident in which one of his best friends fell victim to gun violence: "Nothing's been the same since then. I think Mom only hears what she wants to hear, sees what she wants to see when it comes to her baby brother. Mom knows E.J. is not fine" (35). It has been a year since he dropped out, and he has been making a name for himself as a local deejay rather than make plans to return to school.

Intersectionality and Complex, Fragmented Identities

Through Jade's character, *Piecing Me Together* explores
how multiple identity categories—race, class, gender, size,
ability, and age, among others—come together to form a
singular, unique identity. Intersectionality is a particularly
important concept when it comes to understanding systems
of oppression in the culture—how certain categories of
identity privilege some people and disadvantage others. In
Piecing Me Together, Watson explores blackness,
socioeconomic disadvantage, and girlhood—all identity
categories that may subject an individual to systems of
oppression. Jade's relationships with Sam, Maxine, and Lee
Lee all draw attention to the ways in which intersectional
identity functions, such that the same person can have
different, conflicting dynamics with the same person.
Jade's identity is fragmented, with certain pieces that bond
her to Sam, Maxine, and Lee Lee, and others that drive her
from them.

As African Americans, Jade and Maxine share a common
understanding over race, especially as they have both been
among the few black students in their classes at St. Francis.
However, their socioeconomic differences—Maxine is
from an upper-middle-class background, while Jade is from
a low-income one—makes their experiences of life vastly
different. In contrast, Sam and Jade are both
socioeconomically disadvantaged, but Sam's whiteness
makes her oblivious to racial discrimination, as evidenced
in Chapter 34 when Sam does not see that bias and
stereotypes against black people drove Jade out of the mall
store. Lee Lee and Jade share the same background in
terms of race *and* class, but because Jade has a scholarship
to St. Francis, they are on different paths in life—and

therefore experience their blackness and their class differently.

Jade's collaging and the "fragment" motif seen throughout *Piecing Me Together* reinforce the theme of intersectionality. In Chapter 21, Jade wonders if "a black girl's life is only about being stitched together and coming undone, being stitched together and coming undone. I wonder if there's ever a way for a girl like me to feel whole" (86). This statement alludes to the multitude of categories that make up Jade's intersectional identity and the complex way they interact inside an individual. When the stereotypes and assumptions "rip" Jade apart, she must stitch them back together again, just as she does with her collages.

The Nature of Authentic Mentorship

Well-meaning but flawed mentors and misguided mentorship programs appear throughout *Piecing Me Together*. To best serve Jade and the mentees, Woman to Woman learns to listen to the needs of the mentees so that it functions in a way that truly empowers the girls. By the end of the book, Woman to Woman has undergone a major transformation and achieved a more authentic kind of mentorship: Taking Jade's advice, the organization learns to practice a less condescending form of mentorship, in favor of one that listens to its members' concerns and needs rather than simply try to "fix" them.

While Jade gets real, tangible benefits from the opportunities given to her by Mrs. Parker, she sometimes feels as though she cannot escape them. In Chapter 6, Jade ruminates on the experience of York and Sacagawea, who helped lead Lewis and Clark's expedition; York was a leader on the expedition, but he was nonetheless enslaved.

Paralleling her own experience, Jade wonders "how they [York and Sacagawea] must have felt having a form of freedom but no real power" (24). At the beginning of the book, Jade has freedom, especially with so many "opportunities," but no real power to affect change.

As Jade grows over the course of *Piecing Me Together*, so too does Woman to Woman: What begins as a program that views its mentees as broken people turns into a community-based organization that treats the mentees with dignity and helps them overcome the challenges of navigating a racially biased world. Jade describes the feeling she gets when well-intentioned white individuals want to help her without really listening to her:

> I try to let the music wash away that feeling that comes when white people make you feel special or stupid for no good reason. I don't know how to describe that feeling, just to say it's kind of like cold, sunny days. Something is discomforting about a sun that gives no heat but keep shining (149).

Woman to Woman moves away from this sort of advocacy over the course of the book. For example, in Chapter 39, Woman to Woman takes the girls on an extravagant outing to the symphony where the mentees are subject to stereotyping by a volunteer worker there; by the end of the novel, the organization had taken Jade's suggestion to hold a practical series, called Money Matters, on how to manage personal finances, which is held in a local church in Jade's neighborhood. Another positive change: Jade is empowered by being able to give knowledge to her community, not just receive. This is best exemplified in Chapter 65, when Jade decides she will support Woman to Woman by giving them one of her collages to auction off at a fundraising event: "I like being able to say I'm not just getting an opportunity from Woman to Woman, but that I am helping to keep it thriving. Don't you think that's a good thing?" (233).

The Unique Coming-of-Age Experience for Black Girls

Piecing Me Together underscores how racism in America profoundly shapes the coming-of-age experience for black girls. Racist incidents against African Americans are a constant occurrence in the book. There are incidents that directly involve Jade (for example, when she is confronted in the mall in Chapter 34 and when she is accused of being "unruly" by a lunch lady in Chapter 48); then there is the near-constant background of violence against African Americans in the news, most notably the crime against the black teenager Natasha Ramsey. In Chapter 55, Jade and Lee Lee are terrified when they see a black woman pulled over by a white police officer. For Jade, to grow up as a young black girl in America is to live in terror and a state of constant vigilance, feeling as though she might fall victim or bear witness to violence against African Americans.

Jade also struggles with her relationship to "opportunity," as presented to her by well-meaning white people. As a low-income, black student at St. Francis, Jade is presented with many opportunities by the administrators there, from her involvement in Woman to Woman to SAT prep courses. While Jade does benefit, materially speaking, from these opportunities, she bemoans the exhausting experience of being regarded as an object of pity and a thing to be "fixed." Unlike her white peers or her wealthy black peers, Jade is not able to simply be.

Poverty also shapes Jade's experience growing up. Jade feels as though she needs a "way out" of her current situation, and she recognizes that language can help her realize her dreams: "To give myself a way out. A way in. Because language can take you places" (17). Having been impoverished her whole life, Jade knows that simply working hard will not guarantee her success: "I have never thought about my deserving the good things that have happened in my life. Maybe because I know so many people who work hard but still don't get the things they deserve, sometimes not even the things they need" (58). In this passage, Jade recognizes that racist systems of oppression will never allow her mother to flourish, no matter how hard she works at her multiple jobs.

Jade feels trapped by her rigorous school/mentorship schedule and by the stereotypes that shape people's expectations of her. A desire to be free defines her coming-of-age experience:

> Sometimes I just want to be comfortable in this skin, this body. Want to cock my head back and laugh loud and free, all my teeth showing, and not be told I'm too rowdy, too ghetto. Sometimes I just want to go to school, wearing my hair big like cumulous clouds without getting any special attention, without having to explain why it looks different from the day before. Why it might look different tomorrow (201).

Piecing Me Together concludes with Jade imagining herself alongside the historical figure of York, both of them finally free: "Both of us black and traveling. Black and exploring. Both of us discovering what we are really capable of" (261).

Language

Language is a motif woven throughout *Piecing Me Together*, underscoring themes of self-advocacy, self-exploration, and authentic mentorship. Language appears in multiple forms in the book: There is Jade's enthusiasm for the Spanish language, Jade's father encouraging her to read books, and the idea that Jade is "shy" and needs to learn speak up for herself. "I know Mr. Flores thinks he's preparing us for surviving travel abroad, but these are questions my purpose is asking. I am finding a way to know these answers right here, right now" (49). Language also represents education, as when Jade recalls how her father encouraged her to be a reader: "Dad, I'm serious. You told me that knowing how to read words and knowing when to speak them is the most valuable commodity a person can have. You don't remember saying that?" (74). Education, in this instance, becomes a vehicle for Jade to explore and express herself.

Language also relates to the theme of learning to listen. In Chapter 72, Jade and Sam's reconciliation is put in terms of language and understanding: "When we misunderstand each other, we listen again. And again" (253). Maxine literally silences Jade out of embarrassment in Chapter 41. A moment of weakness and sadness for Jade is marked by an absence of words and an inability to speak: "I don't want an explanation or an apology. That feeling comes again, tightness in chest, tears in eyes. My mouth on lockdown, no words coming out. But they are there; I feel them rising" (166). Jade also frames her freedom in terms of language, using a metaphor involving a tongue: "Sometimes I just want to let my tongue speak the way it pleases, let it be untamed and not bound by rules. Want to talk without watchful ears listening to judge me" (201).

Collage Art

Jade is a collagist and this type of art is a motif throughout the book, meant to underscore and explore the theme of intersectional identity. One of Jade's main motivations of being a collagist is that she can transform the mundane into something sublime: "Tonight I am taking ugly and making beautiful" (25). In bringing together of pieces that do not necessarily fit together, collaging ties into the struggles Jade feels in trying to unite the disparate, sometimes conflicting parts of her intersectional, fragmented identity. In Chapter 21, she explicitly states that being a black girl requires her to endure being "shattered": "But when I leave? It happens again. The shattering. And this makes me wonder if a black girl's life is only about being stitched together and coming undone, being stitched together and coming undone" (86). She makes this reference again when confiding in Maxine that it feels like she is coming apart: "I tell her how I've been thinking about being stitched together and coming undone. 'Do you ever feel that way?' I ask" (214).

The Explorer York

York becomes a symbol for the African American community's finding freedom in self-exploration and expression. York also represents a kind of hope that the success of his descendants—young, black girls like Jade—can right the wrongs of history.

Jade first learns about York in Chapter 6 in a conversation with Lee Lee. Immediately, Jade is taken with the idea of York, and he becomes the focus of many of her collages:

Jade notices a mural of York in Chapter 29, and she takes a picture focused specifically on York: "I take a few photos of the mural. And on the last one, I zoom in on York's face" (118). In Chapter 33, Jade completes her first collage featuring York; it explores the contradiction of her wanting to escape poverty while also loving her community and where she is from. In Chapter 51, Jade asks of York: "Did he even remember being human?" (194). The book concludes with Jade imagining her and York traveling and exploring together, finally free.

Violence Against African Americans

Violence against people of color—particularly, African American people in low-income communities—is a constant backdrop to Jade's life. In Chapter 9, Jade recalls how her uncle E.J.'s best friend was a victim of gun violence: "Like the night E.J.'s best friend, Alan, was killed. Mom kept saying she had this bad feeling, a feeling that something bad was going to happen" (35). Chapter 47 introduces the story of Natasha Ramsey, a 15-year-old black teen who was manhandled by the police at a house party and is in the hospital in critical condition. Later, in Chapter 55, Jade, Lee Lee, and Lee Lee's cousin Andrea come upon a scene in which white cops have pulled over a black woman. They watch fearfully and are relieved when the police give the woman a ticket and release her, but the incident leaves a lasting impression.

IMPORTANT QUOTES

1. "Like the universe was telling me that in order for me to make something of this life, I'd have to leave home, my neighborhood, my friends." (Chapter 2, Page 2)

   Early in the novel, Watson establishes that Jade's primary motivation in life is to escape her social class. This desire presents a moral quandary for Jade: She loves the community she was born into, but she also knows she needs to leave it to achieve success. Woman to Woman, in its approach to advocacy, manifests this contradiction as well.

2. "But girls like me, with coal skin and hula-hoop hips, whose mommas barely make enough money to keep food in the house, have to take opportunities every chance we get." (Chapter 2, Page 7)

   Jade finds it exhausting to be the object of sympathy. She attributes this to her race ("coal skin"), her size ("hula-hoop hips"), and her socioeconomic status ("whose mommas barely make enough money"). As an object of sympathy, Jade needs to be constantly vigilant, and constantly accepting, of any opportunity presented to her.

3. "I think about this as I ride to school. How I am someone's answered prayer but also someone's deferred dream." (Chapter 3, Page 11)

   Referencing the famous Harlem Renaissance writer Langston Hughes, Jade wonders if she is "someone's deferred dream." Jade reflects on her existence on her bus ride to school and views herself as split: On the one hand, her father tells Jade that she is one of the best things that happened to him. On the other, Jade knows that her mother sacrificed so much to raise her.

4. "I think about Mrs. Parker. How she has a black son-in-law smiling at me from a frame. How proud she is of her free passes to Winterhawks games. How she wants me to have a mentor. How she's always ready to give me an opportunity, a gift. Like what she is telling me is she comes in peace." (Chapter 7, Page 26)

    In the previous chapter, Lee Lee told Jade about her history class, in which she is studying Lewis and Clark's role in American history. Jade wonders, when Lewis and Clark presented the Native American tribal leaders with gifts upon first meeting them, if the Native Americans realized that these gifts were "not so innocent" and that the colonists would pillage their land and strip them of their livelihood. In this passage, Jade draws a subtle comparison between her guidance counselor, Mrs. Parker, and the colonists. Jade insinuates that perhaps Mrs. Parker has ulterior motives for offering Jade so many "opportunities" as an underprivileged student at St. Francis.

5. "The light changes. She walks away so fast, I can't ask her what she means by that. Can't ask her what it is she needs." (Chapter 9, Page 31)

    At first, Jade is skeptical of Woman to Woman. Sam, however, thinks that the program sounds great; she remarks to Jade that, through programs like Woman to Woman, at least people notice when Jade needs something, and then she goes on to say that no one ever thinks she needs anything. However, in this scene, before Jade can ask what Sam needs, Sam walks away. It is crucial to Jade to be asked exactly what she needs, and she comes to realize that programs like Woman to Woman are only good insofar as they are addressing real needs. This idea evolves as Jade continues with Woman to Woman.

6. "I don't know what to say to Mr. Franklin. I get it, that he's been here a long time. But I know people who had to move. Mom says it was because the taxes got too high or because they didn't own their homes in the first place. She says people who don't own their homes don't have any real power. I look around Sam's house. She's right: it's small and stuffed and old. But it belongs to them, so that's something. That's a whole lot." (Chapter 12, Page 53)

Jade and Sam have many commonalities on a socioeconomic level, particularly when compared to the wealthy student body at St. Francis. Both girls are from underprivileged, largely impoverished areas of Portland. However, in this passage, Jade notes that, even though the Franklins are poor (their house is "small and stuffed"), as property owners they have a kind of "freedom" that Jade and her family do not have as renters.

7. "There are twelve girls who've been selected for the Woman to Woman mentorship programs. Twelve seeds. Twelve prayers. Twelve daughters." (Chapter 20, Page 79)

Chapter 20 consists of Jade loosely ruminating on the number 12, almost in free-association style. This chapter is an example of the unique way in which the book is written, as fragments that fall outside the main narrative of Jade's life are woven into the structure of the book. It mirrors the collage motif, underscoring Jade's passion for art and her fragmented identity.

8. "I know something happens between the time our mothers and fathers and teachers and mentors send us out into the world telling us, 'The world is yours,' and 'You are beautiful,' and 'You can be anything,' and the time we return to them." (Chapter 21, Page 85)

   Jade has an objectivity borne from her experiences as a young, black girl in an impoverished community. As listens to the advice of the well-meaning wealthy black women of Woman to Woman, she ruminates on how their promises are ultimately empty—the future is not guaranteed for Jade. This discrepancy makes Jade feel disillusioned with Woman to Woman.

9. "I think, *She is not lucky.* She works hard. Figured out a way to keep the lights on and the bills paid. Didn't give up." (Chapter 28, Page 113)

   When Maxine says that Jade's mother is "lucky" for having two jobs, Jade thinks to herself that her mother is not lucky but simply hard-working. This passage highlights the disconnect between Jade and Maxine, whose own mother is a surgeon, while Jade's is a housekeeper/home health worker. Maxine's privilege as an upper-middle-class person creates a blindspot when it comes to understanding Jade's problems.

10. "Maxine is right and wrong. *Those girls* are not the opposite of me. We are perpendicular. We may be on different paths, yes. But there's a place where we touch, where we connect and are just the same." (Chapter 33, Page 132)

Maxine—and, in many ways, the entire Woman to Woman program—is condescending in her approach to the impoverished communities Woman to Woman is intended to help. Jade is sensitive to Maxine's derogatory comments about "those girls"—referring to the majority of Jade's neighborhood peers in North Portland. Jade, however, feels a connection to those girls, and has commonalities with them, that Maxine does not grasp.

11. "The only stores we go into are for skinny girls, so I'm glad I don't have any money to buy anything." (Chapter 34, Page 133)

    One of the key themes in Piecing Me Together *revolves around intersectional identity. In this chapter, Jade accompanies Sam to the local mall, where Jade feels out of place. This passage concisely highlights the way in which two components of Jade's identity—her size and her socioeconomic status—contribute to her marginalization.*

12. "Mom walks to her bedroom. I hear her mumble, 'I've never been to the symphony either.' Her door closes." (Chapter 38, Page 145)

    Jade's involvement in Woman to Woman creates a rift between her and her mother in some ways. When Jade finds out she will attend the symphony with Woman to Woman, her mother is happy for her but also bitter, as shown in the above quote. Jade's mother feels as though the program is "uppity," as she says later; she feels it threatens to make Jade forget the good aspects of her upbringing, her neighborhood, and where she comes from.

13. "'So what, Maxine isn't perfect? This girl graduated from St. Francis as valedictorian. She learned how to navigate this white world, and she's trying to show you how to do the same. You telling me she has nothing to teach you? You better learn how to get from this opportunity what you can and let the rest fall off your back [...] You understand what I'm saying, Jade?'" (Chapter 42, Page 169)

In this passage, Jade's mother angrily forbids Jade from quitting Woman to Woman. Jade is unhappy with the way Maxine treats her, but Jade's mother reminds her that even imperfect people can teach Jade things that are worth learning. Specifically, has learned how to "navigate this white world"; despite the major differences between Jade and Maxine in terms of socioeconomic class, as a black woman Maxine can help Jade learn to navigate a world that privileges white people.

14. "I do not want to be Maxine's [...] charity case, the rebellious backlash against her mother. I do not want her to feel she has to coach me on what to say." (Chapter 41, Page 166)

Chapter 41 marks a major turning point in Jade and Maxine's relationship. When Jade overhears that Maxine is involved in Woman to Woman just because she hopes her work as a "do-gooder" will make her look good to her family, Jade is deeply offended. As she says here, she does not want to be a "charity case" or a "backlash" against Mrs. Winters. This scene is the low point between Jade and Maxine that leads to a significant change.

15. "'Sometimes, Sam, I just want you to listen. Any time I bring up feeling like I'm being treated unfairly because I'm a black girl, you downplay it or make excuses. You never admit it's about race'" (Chapter 54, Page 205)

Jade and Sam have a major argument in Chapter 54 when Sam accuses Jade of being jealous about her going to Costa Rica on the study abroad program. Jade explains that she is not jealous; she is angry and sad at the unfairness of her not having been nominated. Ultimately, Jade voices her main complaint, which is about not being heard: Jade feels as though Sam does not believe that she faces race-related discrimination. This moment is a defining one in Jade and Sam's friendship. Jade finally draws attention to the fact that, while Jade and Sam bond over their shared socioeconomic class, Sam's understanding of race and racial oppression is lacking.

16. "We keep walking. The whole way, I'm documenting the city, taking photos of strangers I've never seen, strangers I see every day. Like the woman who is always sitting on her porch, knitting something." (Chapter 55, Page 208)

Jade sees beauty in the mundane. As she walks around Portland with Lee Lee and Andrea, she takes the casual outing as an opportunity to collect material for her art. With Jade's artistic eye, even an activity as commonplace as knitting becomes a thing of beauty.

17. "Their names are full and vibrant against the backdrop of black sadness. Their names. So many, they spill off the page." (Chapter 56, Page 211)

Jade releases her feelings—intense sadness and frustration over racial injustice, on a personal level and in the world at large—into the collage she creates in Chapter 56. She takes the pictures from an average day with Lee Lee and Andrea and transforms them into a collage that makes a statement on all the "unarmed black men and women [...] who've been assaulted or murdered by the police" (211). Collaging is not only a medium for artistic expression, it is also a vehicle for social justice, as Jade calls the victims "whole and vibrant" (211).

18. "My word comes immediately. *Inspired.*" (Chapter 62, Page 230)

    At the end of the Woman to Woman event at Mia's art gallery, the mentees are asked to close their eyes and think about the art they just saw, letting one word come to mind. Jade's word ("inspired") comes to her almost instantly. This Woman to Woman outing is the first one that truly leaves Jade feeling motivated, marking a significant change in both Jade and the organization.

19. "I get Mom to try a few words. And while I am teaching Mom, she is teaching Maxine what a pinch of that and a dab of this means. While we wait for the food to cook, Mom adds in lessons on love and tells Maxine the remedy to a broken heart. Tells her how to move on. Mom looks at me and says 'You paying attention? You'll need this one day.'" (Chapter 73, Page 255)

    Piecing Me Together *explores the nature of mentorship and finds that it does not come from one type of person or experience. One of the main issues with the kind of mentorship espoused by Woman to Woman (and many other culturally accepted mentorship programs) is that*